Winchester, Virginia: Historical Guide for Travelers

American Cities History Guidebook Series

Henry Church

Published by Fiel LLC, 2023.

While every precaution has been taken in the preparation of this book, the publisher assumes no responsibility for errors or omissions, or for damages resulting from the use of the information contained herein.

WINCHESTER, VIRGINIA: HISTORICAL GUIDE FOR TRAVELERS

First edition. September 11, 2023.

ISBN: 979-8223841791

Written by Henry Church.

Also by Henry Church

American Cities History Guidebook Series
Charlottesville, Virginia: Historical Guide for Travelers
Williamsburg, Virginia: Historical Guide for Travelers
Richmond, Virginia: Historical Guide for Travelers
Norfolk & Virginia Beach: Historical Guide for Travelers
Winchester, Virginia: Historical Guide for Travelers
Baltimore, Maryland: Historical Guide for Travelers
Dover, Delaware: Historical Guide for Travelers
Arlington, Virginia: Historical Guide for Travelers

Table of Contents

Introduction

America's rich history is reflected in Winchester, Virginia, which echoes tales of heroes, eras, and the always changing American narrative. Its roots, which are entwined with the history of the country as a whole, tell tales of tenacity, creativity, hardships, and victories. Winchester is not merely a geographical location to many people; it also serves as a live reminder of America's history and continuing story.

We explore Winchester's complex past in this book, navigating its formative years, significant turning points, and the pulse of its populace. You are taken to a different period or aspect of Winchester's development with each chapter. Walk alongside the early settlers, experience the revolutionary zeal of the populace, observe the difficulties of wars and societal changes, and be amazed at the contemporary innovations and cultural pinnacles that have shaped Winchester's position in the twenty-first century.

Our voyage takes us past the city's architectural wonders, creative legacies, and the economic drivers that fueled its expansion over time. We'll get to know the famous people who made Winchester famous and delve into the societal currents that either began or were bolstered there.

Winchester's story isn't entirely retrospective, though. We will illuminate its present subtleties and consider its future prospects while paying tribute to its past. Readers will gain an understanding of the problems and innovations Winchester is currently facing through this investigation, which also provides information about the direction it might take.

This book offers a thorough and engrossing voyage, whether you're a native of Winchester looking to rediscover home, a history enthusiast eager to uncover its secrets, or a traveler captivated by this American treasure. Join us as we go through the turning points and events that made Winchester, Virginia, the thriving metropolis it is today.

Chapter 1: Native Tribes of Winchester

Winchester, Virginia is located in the Shenandoah Valley, where the Blue Ridge Mountains cast long shadows and the Shenandoah River meanders along a winding course. It is a place rich in history, a nexus of military and cultural events that helped to shape America. However, Native American tribes made this lush valley their home even before the Revolutionary War skirmishes, the Civil War battles, and the apple orchards that would one day dot the area. These tribes' rich and intricate history provides a narrative tapestry that dates back thousands of years before the arrival of the European settlers.

The Eastern Woodlands Native Americans, a group of indigenous tribes, were the first people to live in the Winchester area. The Shawnee and the Tuscarora were two of them, the most powerful tribes in the region, each having their own distinctive set of customs, beliefs, and ways of life. It's also important to remember that other tribes, including the Powhatan and the Delaware, occasionally engaged with this area, usually to engage in commerce or form alliances.

The Shawnee people discovered the Shenandoah Valley to be a favorable region for farming and hunting. They originally came from the western regions of what is now Pennsylvania and Ohio. Being a semi-nomadic tribe, they were adept at taking advantage of the region's abundant natural resources, including the deer, rabbits, and other animals as well as the wide variety of plant species for both culinary and medicinal purposes. The "Three Sisters"—corn, beans, and squash—formed the foundation of their agriculture and were grown in areas that were periodically rotated to maintain soil fertility. Their storytelling, a vital component of their society that passed down knowledge and wisdom through oral tradition through generations, was embellished by their language, a member of the Algonquian linguistic family.

In contrast, the Tuscarora people originated in North Carolina's coastal regions. They were compelled to move as a result of mounting pressure from European settlers, and they found comfort in the Shenandoah Valley's seclusion and unspoiled beauty. Although they had some things in common, such growing maize, the Iroquoian language and customs of the Tuscarora set them apart. Their famed crafts included intricate beading and pottery, which represented both practical utility and spiritual importance. They had an animism-leaning spiritual outlook and thought that every rock, stream, and creature contained some kind of life power. Their ceremonies, many of which were staged to thank the spirits for a bountiful harvest or successful hunt, were punctuated with dance and singing.

The tribes frequently engaged in friendly trade. Archaeological digs near Winchester have uncovered obsidian from distant regions, shells from the Atlantic Coast, and copper from the Great Lakes region, all of which attest to an exchange network that stretched hundreds of kilometers. Even though disputes did occasionally occur, they were usually small-scale and limited, and they were frequently settled by intermarried couples or diplomatic councils.

These tribes also possessed sophisticated systems of government, with councils of elders overseeing the tribe's deliberative procedures. They did not view themselves as landowners in the sense that Europeans did; rather, they considered themselves as custodians of the land. Generosity was valued as a virtue, and communal life was strongly regarded. A successful hunt frequently resulted in a feast for the entire tribe.

Unfortunately, the terrain and future of these Native American tribes were significantly impacted by the entrance of European settlers in the

17th century. Tribes were wiped off by diseases like smallpox, to which the native populace lacked immunity. Land encroachments caused forcible evictions and violent clashes. The Shawnee, Tuscarora, and other tribes were forced further and further west over time, and some of them merged with other tribes in an effort to survive.

The history of these indigenous people is still very much a part of Winchester, yet it is frequently ignored. However, their legacy lives on in the names of neighborhood landmarks, the sustainable farming methods they invented, and the living descendants who continue to reside in the Shenandoah Valley. In fact, following the contours of a pre-colonial America that was as rich in cultural diversity as it was in natural beauty requires traveling back in time to learn more about Winchester's Native American roots.

Chapter 2: Early Settlers and Their Stories

The 17th century began to dawn over the Atlantic, as waves of European emigrants started to head for the "New World." These settlers altered the geography and history of the region where Winchester, Virginia is currently located because they were drawn by the hope of plentiful resources, religious freedom, and the opportunity to start a new life. Although the native tribes had long coexisted peacefully with the land, the advent of the Europeans marked the beginning of a significant—and frequently painful—chapter of cultural conflict and change.

Colonel James Wood, an English immigrant who founded Winchester in 1744, was one of the town's first settlers to have a lasting impact. The Shenandoah Valley's abundant land and advantageous position attracted Wood, who had a land grant from the sixth Lord Fairfax of Cameron, who was also an important landowner in the Virginia colony. Frederick County, which was named in honor of Frederick, Prince of Wales, inspired the original name of the town, which was formerly known as Frederick Town. In honor of Wood's English ancestry, the name was eventually changed to Winchester after the English city of the same name.

But there were difficulties during the town's early years. The European settlers had a different understanding of land use and ownership than the indigenous tribes who had been responsible for maintaining it, which resulted in the enclosing of fields and forests. This created conflict amongst the settlers themselves as well as with the native tribes, especially between the wealthier landowners and the modest farmers who felt more left out.

Many of the original settlers were of German and Scotch-Irish ancestry. The majority of the Scotch-Irish were Presbyterians fleeing Ulster, the most northern region of Ireland, because of economic hardship and religious persecution. The majority of the Germans were Lutherans and Reformed Christians who had been expelled from their homes due to constant fighting and the allure of religious freedom in the colonies. Both groups were eager to carve out their own area in this new world because they considered the Shenandoah Valley's temperature and geography to be similar to their homes in Europe.

Along with their goals and dreams, the settlers carried with them their traditions, languages, and knowledge. For instance, the Germans' introduction of Conestoga wagons and their expertise in crop rotation and animal husbandry significantly advanced local agriculture. The Scotch-Irish, who are frequently given credit for bringing whiskey distillation to America, exploited the region's plentiful supplies of corn and other grains to create alcoholic beverages that would later become deeply ingrained in American society.

Frontier life was a tapestry of struggle and optimism. George Washington, then a young colonel, was stationed in Winchester as a military headquarters for British activities during the French and Indian War (1754–1763). The settlers were constantly in danger of attack, not just from French-allied Native American tribes but also from robbers and other lawless individuals who lived in the chaos of frontier life. During these turbulent times, Fort Loudoun, which was constructed under Washington's direction, acted as a defensive bastion.

But it wasn't all difficulty and conflict. Barn-raisings, quilting bees, and harvest festivals became occasions for social gathering and shared happiness because community was necessary for survival. The daily routine included both music and narrative. European ballads that were brought to America mixed with local rhythms to create wholly

American musical styles. The early settlers made use of the abundant oak and cherry wood to make furniture and converted the local black walnuts into colors.

These early settlers experienced a powerful confluence of uncertainty and opportunity in their daily lives. They built the foundations for the cultural, economic, and social landscapes of contemporary Winchester despite constant obstacles. They permanently altered the Shenandoah Valley through land negotiations, both legitimate and unfair, conflicts that left their mark, and a tenacious will to adapt and succeed.

Although conflict and dispossession disfigured the past, it is also a story of resiliency, innovation, and the unrelenting human drive for a better future. Every cobblestone in the streets of Winchester, every weathered headstone in its ancient cemeteries, and every whispered tale in its folklore bear witness to the countless individuals who, for better or worse, helped to shape the city into what it is today.

Chapter 3: Winchester in the Colonial Era

The second half of the 18th century and the beginning of the American Revolution were a time of significant change for Winchester, Virginia. The town, which is tucked away in the Shenandoah Valley, quickly developed from a little frontier outpost to a vibrant economic and cultural hub. It was a period when wooden pubs were filled with the aroma of pipe smoke, when horses and wagons rumbled over dirt roads, and when the town's ambitions were as high as its churches' towering steeples. The tensions, aspirations, and paradoxes that characterized a new country on the verge of freedom were all there at Winchester, which served as a microcosm of colonial America.

Winchester's creator, Colonel James Wood, could hardly have predicted how crucial it would grow as a strategic hub in the broader scheme of colonial America. The village served as a trading center for commodities like grain, tobacco, and fur due to its location at the junction of numerous Native American trails and European trade routes. It was an excellent position for transportation because of its proximity to the Potomac River. George Washington oversaw the building of Fort Loudoun in 1756, which served as a stronghold for British activities throughout the French and Indian War and significantly increased Winchester's significance. The fort developed into a center for military strategy and a safe haven for settlers fleeing frontier conflicts, laying the foundation for Winchester's long connection to military history.

Winchester's booming economy drew in a wide range of people, giving its social structure additional dimensions. Along the major thoroughfares, merchants, blacksmiths, and artisans established their shops, while farmers from the region brought their harvests to sell in crowded markets. A bewildering variety of items from both sides of the Atlantic were provided by merchants, ever eager to seize opportunities: excellent English fabrics, porcelain from China, spices from the East Indies, and more. Women were also involved in this economic activity as innkeepers, seamstresses, and even traders, a fact that is frequently forgotten in traditional histories.

However, not everyone was able to benefit from the expansion and wealth. A sizable number of African slaves were imported to Winchester to work on tobacco plantations and in domestic jobs because slavery was a pervasive institution. The town's commercial success has a seedy underside caused by their forced labor. The once-free Native American tribes were increasingly pushed to the margins, their territories invaded, and their way of life permanently changed.

Colonial life in Winchester had both religion and education as important components. A number of churches were constructed, including Anglican, Presbyterian, and Quaker congregations, each of which added to the community's moral and spiritual compass. In the beginning, there weren't many schools, and formal education was mostly a privilege for the sons of affluent households. However, as the population increased, so did the need for education, which led to the opening of more schools and even a few lending libraries filled with literary, philosophical, and scientific materials.

The winds of revolution started to blow against this backdrop of economic activity, social inequity, and intellectual ferment. Winchester, a town with significant trade ties to both the colonies and Britain, experienced conflict over independence. Due to its location, it became a hub for political discussion. Taverns and town squares served as venues for passionate speeches for liberty and loyalty. Winchester was a community engulfed in revolutionary fever and ready to add its own chapter to the drama of American independence by the time the first bullets of the American Revolution were fired in 1775 at Lexington and Concord.

Winchester residents joined militias, supplied supplies, and carried out spies operations against supporters of the British government. The town also acted as a treatment facility for injured soldiers, converting churches and public spaces into improvised hospitals. The Winchester area produced notable individuals like Daniel Morgan, a brilliant tactician and sharpshooter who played pivotal roles in pivotal Revolutionary War engagements like Saratoga.

Winchester was therefore a melting pot where Native American, European, and African cultures collided and coexisted during the colonial era. The complex reality of slavery and dispossession brushed elbows with ideals of liberty and self-determination in this setting, where fortunes were earned and lost, where intellectual ideas were argued and spread. Winchester was both a participant in and a spectator to the greater currents of colonial history that determined the fate of a nation. It was a frontier town that evolved into a commercial hub and a haven that evolved into a battlefield. The echoes of that pivotal time may still be heard as one strolls around Winchester's old streets today, serving as a constant reminder of the complex network of people and events that have shaped the city into what it is today.

Chapter 4: Important Landmarks and their History

The city of Winchester is a living, breathing memorial to the ages that have passed over it rather than merely a repository of historical events. The city's structures, streets, and landmarks serve as narrative touchstones, guarding the city's illustrious past in silence. Walking through Winchester is like traveling through time, with each monument providing a fascinating look into the various eras that have influenced this quaint Virginia town's personality.

The Handley Library, a Beaux-Arts architectural marvel that serves as a knowledge citadel, is arguably the most recognizable building in Winchester. The library was created by J. Stewart Barney and Henry Otis Chapman and donated to the city by Judge John Handley, a benefactor from Scranton, Pennsylvania. It served as more than just a location to borrow books when it first opened its doors in 1913; it served as a representation of the community's dedication to learning and intellectual pursuit. Each fresco, each elaborate cornice, even the great staircase that welcomes guests inside, testifies of a bygone era when civic pride was just as important to design as its practicality.

The Old Courthouse, a respectable building located in the center of Old Town Winchester, is also notable. It was built in 1840 to replace an earlier courthouse and has subsequently seen a variety of occasions that have impacted the area. It served as a hospital and a prison throughout the Civil War, and its walls are certainly home to innumerable tales of pain and hope. It now functions as a Civil War museum, with exhibits that serve as a somber reminder of the tumultuous times that once tore the country apart. The Confederate soldier statue in front of the courthouse continues to spark debate and serve as a reminder of the difficulties associated with memory and the passage of time.

Then there is the Stonewall Jackson's Headquarters Museum, which is housed in a Gothic Revival-style villa that previously housed Confederate General Stonewall Jackson's winter headquarters between 1861 and 1862. The museum, which houses an outstanding collection of relics like Jackson's prayer book and his own battle flag, is a miniature representation of the Civil War's history. The cottage provides a close-up view into the life of one of the Civil War's most mysterious people for both history enthusiasts and casual tourists.

With its imposing spire and Georgian design, Christ Episcopal Church adds yet another chapter to Winchester's history. It replaced the earlier wooden structure that had been built in 1738 and was built in 1828. The church has seen Winchester's history in silence as its steeple has watched troops march through the town, new roads being built, and a community growing. Many people who fought against one another in the Civil War but yet frequented the same spiritual haven have warmed its benches over the years.

The oldest house in Winchester, Abram's Delight, provides a peek into life among the early settlers. This limestone home, built in 1754 by Abraham Hollingsworth, has been meticulously restored to its former splendor and now serves as a museum. With period pieces of furniture and artifacts, it provides a fascinating view at the household life and architecture of the 18th century. A recreated blacksmith shop and a log cabin are close by the house, and together they offer more details to the tale of early American life.

Despite being more contemporary, the Patsy Cline Historic House is a captivating monument. This modest home, where country music icon Patsy Cline spent her formative years, has been renovated to look as it did in the mid-20th century. It is evidence of Cline's remarkable rise from a working-class upbringing to become one of music history's most important vocalists.

These landmarks are more than just pieces of construction material; they are the custodians of legends, hopes, and histories. From Winchester's Native American origins and colonial beginnings to its Civil War scars and cultural contributions, they capture the various influences that have created the city. Every historical site acts as a chapter in a book of living history, encouraging us all to read, consider, and recall.

Chapter 5: Winchester during the American Revolution

Winchester developed into a hotbed of political unrest, military strategy, and social upheaval in the turbulent years leading up to and during the American Revolution. Winchester was split as rumors of insurrection against British control spread throughout the 13 colonies, and its citizens became embroiled in a conflict that would ultimately define both the town and the newly forming nation.

Winchester's geographic position gave it strategic significance, making it a suitable gathering place for militias and continental troops as well as a gateway to the western frontier. The city's importance as a hub for trade and transportation only increased. Winchester became the venue for passionate discussions about the advantages and drawbacks of seceding from Britain during the period preceding the revolution. Patriots and loyalists coexisted in the town, albeit under harsh circumstances. They frequently frequented the same pubs and churches and were members of the same families.

Emerging prominent individuals had an impact that went beyond the town's boundaries. One such individual was Daniel Morgan, a shrewd tactician and superb marksman who would win national recognition for his military acumen. Morgan, who was raised in Winchester as a young man while working as a wagoner, was born into a struggling farming family in New Jersey. He became a strong person who was proficient in wilderness survival and battle thanks to the arduous physical effort. The French and Indian War marked the start of Morgan's military career, but it was the American Revolution that would make him famous. He organized Morgan's Riflemen, a group of snipers that was crucial in engagements like Saratoga, which marked a crucial turning point for the Continental Army.

Prior to the development of modern medical facilities, Winchester played a significant role as a hospital town. Churches and public buildings were transformed into improvised hospitals to care for wounded combatants on both sides of the fight. Here, the ladies of the city were crucial, caring for the wounded, sewing bandages, and even helping with surgery. Many of them were caring for patients with illnesses they had never heard of, wounds they had never seen, and sometimes even opponents on the battlefield but suffering companions. Their labor was an exercise in bravery and compassion.

But the darker sides of the revolution also weighed heavily on Winchester's social fabric. Due to increased economic inequality brought on by the conflict, products were scarce and were more expensive. Smuggling spread as locals tried to get over British trade prohibitions. The revolution also further disenfranchised those who were already under oppression. While being denied their own freedom, African slaves were forced to care for the homes and estates of those who were fighting for it. As both the British and Americans sought their support, either by force or dubious treaties, the Native American tribes of the area saw their affiliations put to the test.

The religious institutions of Winchester were likewise forever changed by the revolution. Different denominational clergy members adopted stances, utilizing the pulpit to support or denounce the revolutionary cause. The conflict spread to the churches, where relationships suffered and sometimes families were torn apart due to affiliations. However, the churches also evolved into havens where people went to escape the disorder and violence that had engulfed their lives.

Winchester started the lengthy process of recovery and reconstruction after the Revolutionary War was officially ended by the Treaty of Paris in 1783. Some veterans went back to their old lives, while others were indelibly transformed by the atrocities and victories they had witnessed. The newly constituted American government's economic policies helped the town eventually regain its commercial footing. The revolution's scars and lessons persisted, though, and they entered the cultural memory of Winchester.

Winchester remained a community bound by shared experiences throughout it all, even when those experiences pulled it in different directions. This was true despite the contentious arguments and bitter winters, the smoke of muskets and the tolling of church bells, the sacrifices of its men and the fortitude of its women. The town arose from the American Revolution as a miniature representation of the fledgling country: divided yet united, damaged yet stronger, and permanently branded by an equally intricate and powerful quest for independence.

Chapter 6: Local Heroes and Events of Note

For many years, Winchester has served as a breeding ground for regional figures and occasions that had an impact well beyond its limits. The town has produced people whose deeds and experiences have affected not only Winchester's history, but occasionally the history of the entire country, from its early days as a frontier outpost to its turbulent years during the American Revolution and Civil War, and into the present age. Additionally, it has served as the scene of localized but nationally significant events that have been woven into the fabric of American history.

Let's start with Daniel Morgan, a towering character with deep roots in the Winchester region. Morgan, who is frequently cited as one of the most talented combat strategists of the American Revolution, is known for his tenacity, unbridled skill, and remarkable capacity to motivate the troops he commanded. He returned to Winchester after the revolution as a well-known combat hero and represented the country in Congress. His residence, Saratoga, which was named after the conflict that made him famous, survives as evidence of his ongoing influence.

However, Daniel Morgan was not Winchester's sole military luminary. Admiral Richard E. Byrd, a trailblazing polar explorer who was born in 1888, oversaw missions to the Arctic and Antarctic. According to legend, he was the first person to fly to the North Pole. Byrd's contributions to polar exploration and aviation earned him international acclaim and a place in history, but he was born and reared in Winchester, and he frequently visited the city to share his accomplishments and honors with the people who had raised him.

Unknown but notable individual James R. Graham was an African American educator who started the Douglas School in Winchester. Graham, who was born in 1850 to freed slaves, overcame great obstacles by working tirelessly to give Black students in the segregated South access to educational opportunities. Several generations of African Americans received a decent education from the institution he founded in the late 19th century, enabling them to pursue better chances and throw off the chains of institutional prejudice.

There have also been occasions in Winchester that have drawn national attention. In a campaign rife with them, the battles of Winchester during the Civil War were among the most ferocious. Throughout the conflict, the town changed hands over 70 times, and each occasion was marked by heroic and tragic tales that have been passed down through the generations. In particular, the Battle of Kernstown, a subset of the Battles of Winchester, is renowned for its brilliant tactical execution and tragic loss of life.

Another notable local occasion is the Shenandoah Apple Blossom Festival, which was first held in 1924. What originally began as a modest event to honor the blossoming of apple trees has grown into an annual spectacular that draws tens of thousands of people. The festival, sometimes referred to as "The Bloom," is made up of a variety of parades, concerts, and other activities that not only honor spring but also Winchester's culture, history, and sense of community.

Patsy Cline, a legend of country music who was born and raised in Winchester, rounds out the list. Cline overcame early obstacles like poverty and a lack of a formal education to go on to become one of the 20th century's most significant vocalists. Her music crossed boundaries and transcended genres, and the many aspiring musicians who read about her life found inspiration in it. Her childhood home is now a museum, protecting her history and providing insights into how a music legend is created.

The sinews and muscles that give Winchester its own personality are these individuals and occasions. They act as markers in the history of the community and each have made unique contributions to the rich, multifaceted character that Winchester has today. They serve as a reminder that a place's character is defined not only by its topography and architectural features, but also by the people who rise to meet the challenges of their time and the occasions that best reflect the spirit of the neighborhood. That spirit has always been one of resiliency, inventiveness, and persistent feeling of community in Winchester.

Chapter 7: Post-Revolution Changes and Development

Winchester found itself at the nexus of tradition and progress in the years after the American Revolution. This Virginia community emerged from the war with a mixed sense of triumph and tragedy, togetherness and division, and it too began the difficult process of defining its identity. After the revolution, Winchester underwent significant physical, cultural, economic, and social transformation. These changes and developments also impacted the city's social, political, and economic climate.

The end of the Revolutionary War marked the beginning of an era of economic stability and expansion for Winchester. The town experienced a rebirth in trade and commerce because it was no longer constrained by wartime shortages and the disruptions of military occupation. Its fortunate location close to important east-west and north-south trade routes drew businesspeople, traders, and residents eager to take advantage of a nascent nation's expanding markets. Along the creeks and rivers that wind through and around Winchester, warehouses and mills sprang up, becoming centers of commerce. Along with general stores that sold necessities, the commercial infrastructure ultimately expanded to incorporate more specialized businesses like blacksmith shops, apothecaries, and finally banks.

Transportation advancements were also sparked by the post-war era. The first phase of this renovation was seen in the development and upkeep of roadways. Simple pathways that were earlier traveled became more navigable routes, enabling simpler and quicker transportation of people and commodities. Winchester's economy was boosted as a result of the railroad's introduction in the 19th century, which connected it to markets in the North and South and gradually transformed it into a significant regional hub.

A more organized and visually beautiful design replaced Winchester's haphazard wartime aspect as it started to take shape architecturally. Construction of grand public structures like the Old Courthouse and exquisite mansions that reflected a range of architectural styles from Georgian and Federal to Victorian was spurred on by civic pride and a rising feeling of permanence. Churches also had renovations or were freshly constructed, and the spires of these structures became recognizable elements of Winchester's skyline. These buildings were more than simply bricks and mortar; they represented the aspirations of the neighborhood and served as symbols of its developing identity.

The town's educational institutions expanded along with the town's population and importance. In the years following the American Revolution, a number of schools—both public and private—were established with the goal of giving Winchester's children an all-around education. A significant development was the founding of the Winchester Academy in the early 19th century, which provided a classical education in the humanities and sciences. The establishment of Shenandoah University, which added a higher education institution to the town's educational scene as the century went on, considerably increased the chances for education.

But there were obstacles along the way to growth. As it did over much of the South, the issue of slavery hovered over the town like an ominous cloud. Slave labor played a significant role in the area's agrarian economy, and Winchester was no exception. The community became divided once more as discussions about abolition and states' rights spread across the country, foreshadowing the disputes that would erupt in the Civil War.

Winchester saw a boom in its social and cultural life during this time. Newspapers were created, giving readers access to news as well as articles, poems, and serialized novels for their intellectual enjoyment. Social clubs and civic groups started to appear, providing a forum for community involvement and academic discussion. The popularity of theater, music, and other forms of entertainment raised the level of sophistication in the community's cultural life.

Winchester was able to maintain its distinctive character—a fusion of old values and modern thought—despite all of these changes and advancements. The town, which had formerly been a frontier outpost and a site of conflict, had evolved into a miniature representation of the intricate, diverse country to which it belonged. And while America inevitably proceeded into a new century and fresh difficulties, Winchester also looked ahead, prepared to change, grow, and carry on with its never-ending quest for self-discovery.

Chapter 8: Industry and Infrastructure Growth

Winchester found itself in the midst of an industrial awakening as the 19th century came to a close. The town was infused with a renewed energy and a sense of limitless promise as a result of the development of industry and infrastructure, which was a broad narrative that ran through its veins. A transformation from an agrarian culture influenced by its natural landscapes to an industrial powerhouse designed by human intellect occurred during this time period, marking an epochal change. The changes were both obvious and subtle, impacting Winchester's social structure, physical layout, and cultural imagination in addition to its economy.

The milling and textile industries were some of the first to flourish. Waterways like the Shenandoah River provided mills with a natural resource as well as a logistical benefit. In addition to grinding grains, mills also processed textiles and lumber, making them multipurpose engines of the local economy. For instance, the Shenandoah Woolen Mills grew to be a substantial local employer and developed a reputation for its high-quality, long-lasting products. The number of these factories and mills increased along with the number of related enterprises. The town saw the emergence of tanneries, cooperages, and foundries, each of which added a verse to the industrial symphony now resonating throughout it.

Railroads developed became the arteries of this quickly industrializing body, supplying the commercial center of Winchester with oxygen. The town was connected to the larger economic network of the United States, including the important port cities along the East Coast, when the Winchester and Potomac Railroad was finished. The advent of the train was more than just a technological marvel; it was also a cultural event that captivated the attention of the locals, representing advancement and conjuring up a promising future. Winchester's ability to import and export items with previously unheard-of ease enriched the community and drew additional residents to move there.

Urban infrastructure improvements were triggered by this inflow of new citizens. Public transit alternatives, initially in the form of horse-drawn carriages and subsequently as trolleys, made traveling about the town more convenient. The streets were renovated and widened. Gas lighting lit the nights. A new water system was put in place to take the place of the community's previous haphazard wells and pumps. With the help of numerous subterranean pipes and public works projects, even the less glamorous aspects of urban living, like sewage and trash management, were taken care of.

The demographic makeup of the town underwent a fundamental change throughout the industrial era. Winchester started to become home to people from different backgrounds, including immigrants looking for opportunity, skilled professionals attracted by the prospect of stable employment, and rural residents drawn by the advantages of metropolitan living. Numerous job opportunities were made available by the expanding industrial economy, both in the factories themselves and in the support services that went along with them. The social effects of this were significant, giving rise to early types of workers' insurance and perks as well as labor unions and social clubs.

But the vibrant vitality of industrial development was not without its problems. As rivers grew contaminated and woods became diminished, environmental degradation emerged as an unexpected consequence. The gap between factory owners and employees widened, and some industries experienced difficult working conditions because of the initial lack of labor laws. Grim realities like child labor, lengthy workdays, and a lack of safety precautions have to be accepted.

Even education started to change to meet the demands of an industrial society. Subjects like mechanical drawing, fundamental engineering, and business math were now included in new curriculum. For working people, evening classes were developed, emphasizing the acquisition of practical skills over academic knowledge. As apprenticeships and training programs were developed, schools and colleges began to form ties with nearby businesses, further solidifying the link between education and economic growth.

Newspapers and magazines in Winchester started to reflect this industrial mentality because they were always the heartbeat of the city. Advertisements bragged about the newest equipment, business articles covered market trends, and stories of local business success were told with a sense of community pride. The atmosphere was one of unwavering optimism and a firm faith in the ability of human endeavor to overcome obstacles and control destiny.

And so, Winchester transformed itself into an industrial wonder of its day by a combination of courage and vision, creativity and business. The love for its natural beauty, ties to history, and feeling of community all survived, albeit through a different lens, and it did so without losing its spirit. Winchester proved that infrastructure and business could advance without destroying anything and that pursuing prosperity and maintaining identity were compatible goals. The essential genius of Winchester's industrial era, a period in its history that rang with the clamor of machinery and the whispering of dreams, rested in this precise equilibrium.

Chapter 9: Winchester During the Civil War

Winchester, located in Virginia's Shenandoah Valley, became entangled in the complex web of the Civil War, a turning point in American history. More often than any other town in the United States, the town changed hands more than 70 times throughout the war because of its strategic value to both Union and Confederate armies. Winchester, however, was more than just a tactical chess piece; it was a society ripped apart by ideological conflicts and violent conflict, a town that actively participated in the Civil War rather than simply watching it, its streets, homes, and residents forever changed by the experience.

During the war, Winchester's importance as an economic and transportation hub became a double-edged sword. It became a hub of military operations because the same roads and railroads that had fuelled its economic development now made it easier to deploy troops and supplies. Confederate and Union forces competed for control of Winchester as the war got under way because they knew that whomever secured the town would have sway over the whole Shenandoah Valley and its vital resources. The town's tranquil surroundings were transformed into bloody battlegrounds by engagements like First and Second Winchester, Kernstown, and Opequon.

Winchester started to see frequent occupations, and each change in power brought with it a unique set of difficulties for the locals. The next day, Union soldiers would march through the city, enforcing their own set of laws and requisitioning goods while Confederate flags would flap on rooftops and Southern music would fill the air the day before. Whatever their political views, the citizens confronted the trials of damaged property, confiscated resources, and an ever-present sense of dread. Unpredictability and stress were their constant companions.

The war also made people more human. To provide care for the injured soldiers on both sides, hospitals were built in churches, public spaces, and private residences. As local women and men, especially nuns from the nearby Catholic church, became nurses and carers, the histories of these medical facilities are infused with tales of compassion and sorrow. The experience of the Confederate physician Hunter Holmes McGuire, who rose to fame for his cutting-edge surgical techniques and his unwavering devotion to his patients, best captures Winchester's medical history during the Civil War.

The demography of the town significantly changed as the conflict continued on. Women, children, and the elderly were left to handle families and enterprises after many men left to fight. The deeply rooted institution of slavery in Winchester and the surrounding area started to disintegrate. While some enslaved people stayed, unsure of what freedom might look like in a war-torn continent, others took advantage of the instability to flee, seeking freedom beyond Union lines or farther north.

Social dynamics changed as a result of the continuous hostilities. Families were frequently compelled to provide food and shelter to soldiers, sometimes voluntarily and other times under coercion, which put the traditional Southern hospitality to the test. Churches evolved into not only places of worship but also social and political platforms, and occasionally even improvised hospitals or barracks. The distinctions between civilian and military life became more hazy, and day-to-day life began to resemble a struggle and shared sacrifice.

Education was affected as well. Regular school closings occurred, which disturbed educational norms. The war was a formative event for the Winchester children, who watched with impressionable eyes images of bravery and sorrow that would live in their memory forever.

Despite the psychological and physical costs, Winchester's community managed to endure and even push back. Through sewing groups, food preservation, and volunteer work, women assumed more significant responsibilities in supporting households and helping with the war effort. Some locals engaged in covert espionage and subterfuge, supporting their favoured side through data collecting and covert acts of sabotage.

When the war was finally over in 1865, Winchester came back, scarred but standing, like a phoenix. A fresh set of difficulties and opportunities emerged during the Reconstruction era that followed, but that is a topic for another chapter. Winchester had undergone significant transformation as a result of the Civil War, including changes to its economy, social structure, and very identity. But it had also demonstrated the fortitude and tenacity of its people. The town had served as a reflection of the greater national battle, but in that reflection could be seen the distinctive features of Winchester's own sons and daughters, who had survived, fought in, and lived through one of the most turbulent periods in American history. A tribute to human resiliency in the face of great adversity, their experiences are intertwined into the vast story of the Civil War and are permanently imprinted into the very character of contemporary Winchester.

Chapter 10: Reconstruction and its Impact

Winchester, like the rest of the South, was pushed into the unfamiliar and difficult world of Reconstruction just as the fires of the Civil War were beginning to simmer. Winchester struggled with its own process of physical and societal healing while the United States tried to put itself back together after a horrific conflict. This time, which lasted from 1865 through the late 1870s, was not just a period of rebuilding and making amends; it was also a test of the community's fortitude, ideals, and sense of solidarity. Infused with new norms, defined by the entry and departure of people and institutions, and scarred by the repercussions of conflict, the town emerged from this revolutionary era radically altered.

Following the Civil War, the practical issue of physical reconstruction was the main priority. Businesses needed to be revived, war-damaged buildings needed to be repaired or rebuilt, and the area's agricultural economy, which supported the community, demanded immediate attention. Federal initiatives, such as help from the Freedmen's Bureau, were helpful in certain ways but frequently mired in bureaucracy and political wrangling. Local individuals took it upon themselves to reconstruct their area, frequently utilizing private initiatives, regional support networks, and resourcefulness from the area. Soon enough, the warehouses were refilled, the mills started to turn once again, and Winchester's economic pulse returned to normal.

The alteration of the social fabric, particularly with regard to racial relations and the newly freed African American population, was the most significant and contentious topic, though. Although emancipation began a new chapter, the prevailing social standards did not change overnight. The difficult job of establishing lives as free citizens in a society that had not yet overcome its deeply rooted biases lay before African Americans, many of whom had been held as slaves in Winchester and its surroundings. Even though the Freedmen's Bureau and a number of religious institutions provided educational and employment possibilities, the road to full equality was difficult and protracted. With regards to voting limitations, segregated schools, and constrained economic possibilities, discrimination continued.

New political dynamics were also implemented during the Reconstruction period. Winchester had to negotiate a difficult and frequently tense relationship with federal authorities because the South was first under military occupation. As former Confederates were disenfranchised and then gradually permitted back into the democratic system, political power frequently changed hands. The time was characterized by heated discussions, election excitement, and a sizable amount of civil upheaval. The town square once again served as a stage for the town's collective consciousness to express its hopes, anxieties, and conflicts at various moments when Winchester became a focal point for political rallies, protests, and meetings.

New social institutions and organizations emerged during this time, while others changed. The church continued to be a strong power, but it occasionally experienced racial and political division. In order to adapt educational institutions to the demands of a post-war society, former slaves were integrated into public schools, albeit in a segregated way. Civic groups, many of which had been put on hold or used for other purposes during the war, reclaimed their original purposes, supporting philanthropic endeavors, educational initiatives, and community improvement initiatives.

The media environment changed as well during Reconstruction. Newspapers, which had previously served as channels for propaganda during times of conflict, now serve as social watchdogs and venues for public discussion. With its own set of biases and conflicts, the journalistic narrative changed from one of conflict to one of reconstruction. Public perceptions of Reconstruction policy, local administration, and changing social values were significantly shaped by these media.

Winchester's economy started to diversify. Agriculture continued to play a significant role in the town, although small-scale manufacturing and trade both increased. Originally used to transport military supplies, the railroad now serves as a vital link for commercial goods, connecting Winchester to larger markets and aiding in its slow and rocky return to pre-war prosperity.

By the time Reconstruction officially ended in the late 1870s, Winchester had undergone a transition that affected all element of life, including its physical streets and buildings as well as its social standards and governmental structures. This time period left behind a complex history of development and opposition, successes and failures, and unification and division. Winchester, though, had also discovered a means to remake itself, to adapt to new realities while maintaining its essential essence. Winchester had been put through a crucible during the Reconstruction era, and it had come out the other side both scarred and stronger, a community ready to move on while yet being firmly rooted in the past.

Chapter 11: Winchester in the Gilded Age

Winchester found itself mirroring the larger currents of American society—industrialization, urbanization, and the quick change in social and political norms—as the country entered the Gilded Age, roughly from the late 19th to the early 20th century. The Gilded Age was a period of opposites, and Winchester was no exception. It was named for the glimmering surface wealth that concealed profound societal disparities. Here was a community that was ready to seize the opportunity of modernity and progress while still recovering from the effects of the Civil War and Reconstruction.

Winchester saw industrialization, but it happened in a way that was appropriate for its setting and natural advantages. Winchester experienced the expansion of industries that complemented its pre-existing agricultural foundation, as opposed to the large-scale manufacturing that sprang up in Northern cities. The terrain started to be dotted with flour mills, tanneries, and other manufacturing businesses that processed materials from the neighborhood. In the fertile Shenandoah Valley, apple orchards grew profusely, giving Winchester a new moniker as the "Apple Capital of the World." The development of the apple processing sector, which transformed Winchester into a hub for apple-related products, from cider to apple sauce, was possibly the best example of the blending of agriculture and industry.

The town's appearance changed as a result of urbanization, another feature of the Gilded Age. The building of large residences, frequently in the newest architectural designs, signaled newfound affluence and a growing social stratification. Victorian mansions served as the residences of wealthy businessmen and industrialists, with their elaborate woodwork and turrets signifying the aspirations and accomplishments of a developing upper class. The rising numbers of workers and clerks were housed in neighborhoods with more modest homes. The commercial areas of Winchester also developed, with a variety of stores, hotels, and even theaters springing up to cater to a growing population.

During the Gilded Age, civic improvements were another priority. Public services were put into place, including basic sanitation systems, police, and fire departments. Schools grew in size, and education started to be seen as a pillar of civic virtue. Women's clubs and civic groups thrived, frequently serving as the catalyst for social change and humanitarian initiatives. For instance, these associations frequently spearheaded activities that led to the creation of libraries and public parks. With the construction of better roads, the growth of the railroad, and the introduction of utilities like gas and later electricity, infrastructure also witnessed modest advancements.

The surface of wealth and advancement, meanwhile, was unable to completely hide the underlying societal problems. As industrialization brought about a new set of working circumstances that were frequently unfavorable, labor disputes were not uncommon. As wealth gaps widened, a class system that reflected the greater American society emerged. Race relations, which were still raw from the Civil War and Reconstruction eras, simmered on the surface. Even though African Americans had achieved great achievements in employment and education, segregation was still the norm, and the threat of injustice persisted in numerous ways.

Political unrest was also prevalent during the Gilded Age. In the neighborhood newspapers and taverns, there was a lot of discussion about tariffs, monetary policies, and the balance of federal and state authorities. Parties and politicians battling for control of the narrative made local politics frequently a microcosm of the national stage. Winchester also experienced its fair share of fascinating individuals, including industrial tycoons, charismatic politicians, and even snake-oil salesmen, all of whom added to the rich tapestry of life at this time.

Winchester started to become its own in terms of culture. The rise of neighborhood newspapers, lecture series, and social organizations that discussed anything from literature to science enhanced the historical and intellectual life of the neighborhood. Churches served as social and political hubs in addition to meeting spiritual needs as religion continued to play a significant role in society. Winchester became a more multicultural location than its population would suggest as a result of the emergence of new musical, dramatic, and creative groups.

The legacy of the Gilded Age—a complex mash-up of development and concerns, of shining accomplishments and unresolved problems—came with Winchester as it entered the 20th century. This was a community that had been altered by the forces of industry, social development, and modern aspirations while remaining firmly planted in its past. The individuals who called Winchester home were the most permanently affected by the era, though the streets and architecture also bore its imprint. Their experiences, which frequently mirrored the more significant victories and setbacks of the American Gilded Age, constituted an essential element of the town's intricate, always changing narrative.

Chapter 12: The Rise of Technology and its Effects

Few things had a greater impact on Winchester's development during the 20th century's enormous tapestry of change than the development of technology. This time period marked a fundamental shift in people's work styles and productivity, as well as in the basic fabric of daily life, affecting everything from communication and entertainment to transportation and medicine.

The development of the railroads and the spread of the telegraph led to the first waves of technological innovation. Despite having their roots in older eras, these systems had advanced significantly by the early 20th century. Railroads weren't simply moving people and cargo; they were also transporting industrial materials, consumer items, and even cultural influences. The telegraph system accelerated information flow, as did the development of telephone lines. The links between Winchester and the rest of the world have become more tightly knit as news that used to take days to reach us now arrives in minutes.

Automobiles transformed urban planning and personal mobility. Model Ts and later, more sophisticated automobiles replaced horses and carriages. The suburban expansion made possible by the car increasingly complemented, and eventually threatened, the primacy of Winchester's downtown area. Over time, the logic of the vehicle changed Winchester's geography as roads were paved, widened, and street signs were put up.

Electricity revolutionized both homes and businesses. Electric lighting now shone where gas lamps and candles formerly flickered. factories that used steam power or manual labor started switching to electric machinery. This affected the patterns of life fundamentally; it wasn't merely a matter of convenience or effectiveness. People were not constrained by the setting sun and could work and socialize well into the night. Electric equipment, from refrigerators to washing machines, sparked a domestic revolution in homes that had a profound effect on women's lives by freeing up time that had previously been devoted to household duties.

Significant progress was also made in communication technologies. By the 1920s and 1930s, radios had become commonplace, acting as a gathering place for families to listen to music, news, and serialized dramas. Newspapers, a mainstay of Winchester's informational diet for many years, had to contend with these immediate broadcasts. Then the invention of television further changed how people in Winchester absorbed media and perceived their place in the world.

Many of these developments were welcomed with enthusiasm, but they also raised important queries and worries. For instance, labor-saving technology frequently led to the displacement of workers, especially in established industries that were unable to quickly adapt. Additionally, the vehicle culture that altered Winchester's geography also contributed to pollution and urban expansion issues, changing not only the community's physical layout but also its environmental health. Additionally, the mass media's amplification of American culture started to homogenize it, with regional traditions and stories occasionally being swamped by national trends and voices.

Education and healthcare were two more areas where technology had an impact. Projectors and computers were first incorporated into the curricula in Winchester schools. Although this also sparked continuous discussions about educational inequality because not all schools or students had equal access to these materials, classrooms became more dynamic and engaged settings. In the field of healthcare, technological advancements allowed Winchester's hospitals to frequently conduct surgeries that formerly required a journey to a big metropolis. The health of the community was revolutionized by advances in diagnostic technology, novel medications, and a more methodical understanding of public health.

The development of technology was not entirely a good thing, either. Winchester became increasingly susceptible to outside shocks, such as economic downturns, energy crises, or cyberthreats, as a result of the complexity and interconnection of technical systems. Concerns regarding mental health and social cohesiveness have also arisen as a result of the accelerated pace and pressure of a technologically advanced society. As people grew increasingly absorbed in their own devices, traditional places of community contact, such as church gatherings, town meetings, and social clubs, saw a fall in attendance. However, new communities also developed as a result of civic organizations organizing online or as a result of regionally specific websites and social media platforms that kept Winchester inhabitants informed and involved.

By the turn of the twenty-first century and the beginning of the twenty-first, Winchester had undergone yet another transformation, this time brought on by circuits, silicon, and the constant hum of data streams. But the town's essential character remained unchanged, just as it had in earlier times. The superficial aspects of life had been greatly altered by technology, but Winchester's persistent ideals, difficulties, and sense of community kept its residents motivated. The problems of fairness, purpose, and connection that humans have always had persist despite the advancement of technology. Winchester entered the digital era with the wisdom of its history, using new means to solve age-old problems and coming up with creative ways to celebrate its shared joys.

Chapter 13: Winchester during WWI and WWII

The First and Second World Wars were not just distant happenings that Winchester residents read about in the newspapers or heard on the radio; they were epochal shifts that changed the town's social structure, economy, and even its physical landscape.

America's entry into World War I in 1917 was greeted in Winchester with a mixture of trepidation and patriotic zeal. World War I was the country's first big military intervention on foreign land in the 20th century. The town's resources and inhabitants were swiftly mobilized by the battle. Men enlisted or were drafted into the military, reporting to training facilities before to deployment. Those who stayed behind devoted themselves to fighting the battle at home. Backyard victory gardens grew, Liberty Bonds were bought and sold, and women donned work clothes to labor in factories or volunteer for the Red Cross.

Winchester, which is a small town, experienced the effects of a world at war. Local businesses changed their production strategies to aid in the war effort. For instance, the orchards that had previously served as the foundation of the neighborhood's economy found new use as suppliers of canned apples and other food items for military rations. As women and African Americans began to fill roles that had previously been the sole preserve of white men, the social fabric of Winchester also underwent a transformation that paved the way for more significant societal upheavals.

1918's armistice offered both relief and significant changes. Soldiers who returned brought with them experiences that would forever change them, frequently in ways that the town could neither fully understand nor effectively treat. The "Lost Generation" had lost its innocence abroad, but it had also acquired a global outlook that would shape Winchester's politics and culture for years to come.

World War II was a seismic upheaval if World War I was a rupture. Young men from Winchester once more heeded the call to duty and served in a variety of war zones, from the islands in the Pacific to the sands of North Africa. However, the war effort this time was far more extensive, with an almost industrial level of planning and organization. On an unprecedented scale, local factories were converted for the war effort, producing equipment and supplies that were essential to the military. Along with joining the economy in large numbers, women also filled auxiliary positions in the armed services. Incorporating the collective sacrifices that defined the American experience during the war, Winchester's citizens' contributions on both the home front and the battlefield were woven into the wider national story.

There were considerable demographic changes after World War II. People from all backgrounds, including immigrants from other areas of the country, were drawn to Winchester by the economic opportunities provided by the wartime businesses. As a result, the town's racial and cultural diversity increased. As the war came to a conclusion, soldiers started to return home with new skills, GI Bill benefits for college, and a determination to change their lives and the community.

In addition to hastening social transformation, the wars also made societal injustices that had been boiling apparent. African Americans who had heroically served their country in the military were welcomed back to a segregated and racist society. After experiencing professional life, women were now urged to revert to household responsibilities, which helped pave the way for the feminism movements of the 1950s and 1960s.

Winchester's actual physical environment was likewise irrevocably changed. Roads and public buildings, among other infrastructure, were constructed or renovated during the war years and served as the town's skeleton for post-war growth. Due to the experience of global conflict, community planning and civil defense had a renewed feeling of urgency, which prompted the development of more structured and effective local government systems.

The GI Bill permitted a boom in housing and education in the years following World War II, transforming the social and economic calculus for many families. Many veterans used their educational benefits to attend college or learn a trade, which allowed them to advance into the growing middle class. Around Winchester, suburban communities started to prosper, following a national trend toward the suburbs.

Winchester had changed by the time the smoke had cleared and the world had come to a tenuous peace. It was more than just a small Virginian hamlet; it served as a microcosm of all of America's struggles and victories throughout the most volatile time in contemporary history. Global warfare had expedited Winchester's evolution and put it to the test, having a lasting effect on future generations. Winchester was guided by the fundamental values of community and resiliency as it navigated the challenging post-World War II environments.

Chapter 14: Military Bases and Economics During WWII

Intense and extensive mobilization brought on by World War II changed not just military tactics but also economic foundations. The same was true in Winchester. The development and operation of military bases and supply depots in the region served as a catalyst for the town's metamorphosis into a key node in the military-industrial complex. These facilities supported the local economy in a mutually beneficial way: the military required the labor and resources that Winchester could offer, and in return, the town profited from the jobs, economic expansion, and technological improvements.

Following the attack on Pearl Harbor in 1941, the United States immediately prepared to enter the war by transforming existing places into regions that could aid in the war effort. Existing factories switched from making consumer items to generating supplies for the war. Apples were originally grown on those fields, but now they were used for practice. Even neighborhood schools and public buildings provided space for community mobilization and civil defense measures.

One of the most major changes was the opening of a supply depot close to Winchester with the intention of supplying supplies and equipment to military installations throughout the East Coast and even to soldiers serving abroad. Hundreds of locals and others who came to Winchester in search of work were employed by the station, which grew to be a center of activity. The reverberations were tangible. There was a boom in house building, a spike in retail, and an increase in services like banking, healthcare, and transportation as a result of so many people moving to the area. The infusion of people and money made the local economy stronger and more varied than it had, if ever, been before.

Social developments went hand in hand with the economic ones. Military bases and depots frequently recruited an ethnically and racially varied workforce, resulting in a mingling of communities and cultures. This blending presented both a chance and a challenge. Although it strengthened Winchester's social structure, it also exposed hidden racial and gender imbalances. During a large portion of World War II, the military was segregated, and this segregation was replicated in civilian life. This created tensions that would peak during the Civil Rights era. Similar to how males were driven back into more traditional roles after returning from war, women also took on jobs and roles that were historically held by men.

The transfer of technology from the military to the civilian sector also had an enduring effect. Technologies that were once created for use in battle now have uses in peacetime. For instance, improvements in engineering, logistics, and communications trickled down into the neighborhood's economy, giving Winchester firms a competitive edge throughout the years following the war. Long after the war was over, the town continued to benefit from the roads and bridges that were constructed or upgraded during the war years.

The advantages, though, came at a price. Because they required land and resources, military outposts occasionally damaged regional ecosystems and customary ways of life. Apple orchard-focused farmers discovered that their grounds had been repurposed, permanently changing their daily routines. Additionally, Winchester was susceptible to post-war economic changes due to the concentration of economic activity around the military. After the war, when military bases shrank or shut down, the community had to fill the economic void they left behind.

Military installations also influenced Winchester's sense of civic duty. The post-war civic initiatives ranged from the founding of veterans' groups to more commonplace but significant initiatives like neighborhood beautification programs and educational reforms. The war had created a communal sense of responsibility and sacrifice, feelings that found expression in post-war civic activities. The common struggles of the war years gave rise to a communal ethos that went beyond personal goals for many people, producing a group identity that would have an impact on Winchester's social and political life for decades to come.

Winchester has gone through significant and subtle changes by the end of World War II. It had grown in size, character, and technological sophistication. The military installations that were largely responsible for this change were ostensibly centered on international conflicts that were far away from this Virginia town, but their impact was primarily local and changed the course of Winchester's development in ways that would reverberate throughout the subsequent chapters of its history.

Chapter 15: Winchester in the Civil Rights Era

The racial dynamics in Winchester during the Civil Rights Era must be understood in the context of a city with a rich history. The city had served as a key military location throughout the Civil War, and the remnants of a split country were soaked into its streets. The city, mirroring the country, saw a tremendous upheaval during the 1950s and 1960s, and the social wounds of the past provided both barriers to change and avenues for it.

Winchester's first reaction to the famous Brown v. Board of Education decision was less than favorable, as it was throughout in the South. The local school board decided on a course of "massive resistance," which was supported by Virginia's political elites who wanted to get around the federal desegregation laws. However, the African American community's tenacity and the growth of regional Civil Rights organizations started to put strain on these accepted practices. Young and old activists planned freedom rides, staged sit-ins at segregated restaurants, and conducted voter registration drives. The combined efforts of Winchester activists reflected the national struggle for Civil Rights into the city's distinctive historical environment, much like the exquisite designs of the stained glass windows in its famed Handley Library.

While public places like libraries, swimming pools, and movie theaters continued to be segregated, the African American community came up with creative ways to challenge the old quo. Older community members taught younger generations not only reading and math skills but also the history of their ancestors in the church basements, giving them the knowledge and skills they would need to challenge and demolish the segregated society they had inherited.

During this time, notable individuals rose to prominence, adding to Winchester's illustrious past. One of them was Reverend Douglas Griffin, a local African American church's pastor who rose to prominence as a proponent of desegregation and social change. His sermons served as rallying cries for activism in addition to spiritual elevation. Griffin's home and church served as frequent gathering places for planning demonstrations and debating the appropriate legal measures to challenge local laws enforcing segregation.

The immovable barriers of discrimination eventually started to crumble. The desegregation of the nearby John Handley High School was one of the most telling examples. This was more than simply a school's integration; it marked a turning point in society's long-standing social barriers. A modest but substantial shift in the city's common awareness occurred when local newspapers that had previously supported racial stereotypes began to report the Civil Rights Movement more objectively.

The Civil Rights Movement had significantly altered Winchester by the late 1960s. To think that the fight was over, though, would be foolish. Legal segregation was abolished, but the city still had to deal with concerns like economic inequality and covert racial prejudice, which are still relevant today as Winchester develops.

Winchester's experience during the Civil Rights Era was integral to its ongoing path and inextricably connected to the wider American story. It was far from an isolated chapter in Winchester's history. The city, with its colorful heritage and intricate social fabric, both absorbed and mirrored the desire for justice and equality that throughout the country. The legacy of this time period is still being dealt with by Winchester, just like the rest of America, guaranteeing that the story is far from over and adding yet another intricate layer to its already rich past.

Chapter 16: Other Notable Social Movements in Winchester

The numerous social movements that peppered Winchester's history served as the carving tools, gradually forming the city's character and social dynamics, if the Civil Rights Era served as the furnace that challenged the city's moral and social fiber. These movements made a substantial contribution to the complex mosaic that is today's Winchester, even if they may not have been as revolutionary as the fight for racial equality.

Winchester's tradition of strong matriarchs and female business owners contributed to the Women's Suffrage Movement's unexpected success in this Virginian metropolis. While many suffragists concentrated their efforts in large cities, a group of women in Winchester believed that their town was ready for change. These women started to engage the neighborhood in conversations about voting rights and gender equality by utilizing the social ties they had made at church events and civic organizations. Mary Wilson, a notable activist and native of Winchester, launched grassroots campaigns by taking use of her standing in the city's elite social circles. Her home turned into a sanctuary for covert gatherings where strategies for influencing local politicians were developed. They also planned educational activities to raise awareness of suffrage as a crucial human right among women and the general public. When the 19th Amendment was ultimately ratified in 1920, it was celebrated locally as well as nationally with parades down Winchester's cobblestone streets.

The environmental movement, which gained traction in the latter decades of the 20th century, was another fascinating societal undercurrent. Winchester's inhabitants have always had a symbiotic relationship with the natural world because of the city's closeness to the Shenandoah Valley and the Appalachian Mountains. However, the pure beauty of the surrounding landscapes started to be threatened by industrialisation and urban growth. To defend their cherished valley, environmentalists and conservationists banded together, frequently cooperating with national organizations. The Winchester Green Circle is a network of trails and paths that was started as a result of community-based campaigns to raise environmental awareness. The movement resulted in a collaboration between public and private stakeholders and ultimately had an impact on regional land use and conservation regulations.

Indelible traces of the LGBTQ+ rights movement may also be seen across Winchester's social landscape. Despite the city's reputation as a traditionally conservative place, in the late 20th and early 21st centuries, there was an increase in the acceptance of different gender identities and sexual orientations. Activists in Winchester took up the cause for LGBTQ+ rights as a result of national landmarks like the Stonewall riots and the legalization of same-sex marriage. As community organizations and gay-straight alliances in schools began to form, secure environments for debate and advocacy were established. The Shenandoah LGBTQ Center developed into a pillar organization over time, offering tools and community outreach that were unthinkable in past decades.

Each of these movements added to the social and historical fabric of Winchester. Today, women like Mary Wilson are honored for their contributions to society as well as their role as matriarchs. The Winchester Green Circle is more than just a hiking trail; it serves as a symbol of the town's dedication to environmental protection. More than just a structure, the Shenandoah LGBTQ Center serves as a benchmark for the progress the community has made in embracing diversity and human rights.

These movements contributed to Winchester's transformation into a more open and progressive city; they were more than just historical footnotes. Their tales, which are weaved throughout the story of Winchester, provide engrossing insights into the complex social processes that have defined the character of the city. Like the city itself, these movements are also constantly changing, with repercussions that are still felt today and the potential to shape Winchester's future. In essence, the story of Winchester's involvement with numerous social organizations is a mirror of larger American themes—of struggle, change, and an unwavering goal for a more equal society—as well as an explanation of its particular features.

Chapter 17: Technological Revolution of the 20th Century to the Millennium

Unprecedented developments were in store for Winchester and the United States both at the turn of the 20th century. As the century progressed, it became obvious that technology would serve as the catalyst for change, profoundly influencing every facet of society, from industry and communication to education and healthcare. Winchester served as both a participant in and a beneficiary of this technological revolution between the early 1900s and the start of the new millennium, acting as a microcosm of the tectonic transformations taking place across the country.

The coming of the railroads was a significant turning point for Winchester, notably in the area of industry. The Winchester and Western Railroad, afterwards the Baltimore and Ohio (B&O) Railroad, completely changed the city's economy. These railroads made it simpler for products like apples, a crucial crop for the area, to go to distant markets. Winchester's advantageous location close to Washington, D.C., and other significant Eastern cities served as a catalyst for industrial development. The wealth of the local agricultural industry and the better transportation systems quickly led to the emergence of factories.

The technological aspirations of Winchester grew as the 20th century went on. The age of automation and mechanization would not leave the metropolis behind. Winchester had developed into a center for manufacturing by the middle of the 20th century, with industries using cutting-edge equipment for more productive production. In many of these industries, the advent of the assembly line heralded a departure from traditional forms of manual labor, a revolutionary development that reflected broader changes in the American workforce.

Winchester's establishment of facilities by businesses like Kraft Foods and General Electric is an example of the city's fusion into the industrial age of mass production.

Additionally, communication technologies have a significant impact on the city. Winchester was more interconnected than ever before with the rest of the nation as a result of the widespread use of telephones and later the growth of television networks. Local media benefited from these developments. Radio and television stations started to compete for audience attention with newspapers, which used to be the main source of information. The Internet and personal computers started to become more prevalent as the century came to an end. Public institutions like libraries and schools adopted these new technologies, strengthening their instructional programs and repurposing them as hubs for digital literacy.

The technology tsunami also affected the healthcare industry in Winchester. As X-ray machines, ultrasound technologies, and computerized record-keeping became more widely used in hospitals, medical practice changed from an art of educated guesses to a science of accuracy. In reality, the Winchester Medical Center rose to prominence as a pioneer in the region for medical technology, luring talent and funding that would have appeared unlikely earlier.

The evolution of education was also amazing. As early as the late 1980s, Winchester Public Schools started integrating computers into its curricula. By the 1990s, the Internet had made its way into schools, creating a whole new world of educational tools. The Handley Library, a fortress of conventional education, quickly changed to keep up with the changes by adding computer labs and online resources, ensuring its continued relevance in an increasingly digital world.

The technological revolution was a societal change as well as one involving machines and devices. In addition to moving things, the railroads also moved ideas, connecting Winchester to the outside world and integrating it into a larger national dialogue. The factories served as both production hubs and microcosms of societal development, capturing changes in both economic and labor dynamics. Communication innovations not only made the world smaller but also completely changed how Winchester residents interacted with one another and their neighborhood. Each new technological development expanded the parameters of what was feasible for both people and Winchester as a whole.

Winchester was on the cusp of a new era as the 20th century gave way to the 21st. The twentieth century's technical developments had prepared the way for a world that was much more complicated and linked. The occupants were forced to reinterpret their place in this quickly changing environment because the transition was not only physical but existential as well. In this way, Winchester's technical revolution can be seen as a chapter in the larger story of American innovation and adaptability, a story that is still being written as we speak.

Chapter 18: Changing Demographics and Culture of the 20th Century to the Millennium

Each century in the history books has its own distinct mark—a fusion of innovations, wars, movements, and individuals—that characterizes it. However, if one were to pick just one word to describe how the 20th century played out in Winchester, Virginia, it might be "transformation." But when one considers the enormous changes in demographics and society that took place from the early 1900s to the new millennium, even this word would appear inadequate. It appears as though the city has seen a number of rebirths, each with its own unique fusion of cultures, traditions, and standards.

Winchester was mostly a small agricultural town in the early 20th century, and the local economy was strongly dependent on the nearby farms and apple orchards. But the city started to change as the century went on. The Great Migration, a nationwide movement that saw millions of African Americans leave the Southern states in search of better opportunities in the North and West, brought about the first big transformation. Winchester saw an increase in its African American population despite not being a popular travel destination. New churches, companies, and community groups that catered to the expanding population were founded as a result of the change that provided culture and energy.

Second World War onset sparked yet another change. People were drawn to industrial production from rural areas and smaller towns, resulting in a workforce with a wider range of socioeconomic status and life experience. Winchester's expanding variety gained even another dimension as a result of the inflow of military troops and their families both during and after the war. During this time, more women entered the workforce, changing their traditional roles as domestic helpers to those of contributors to the economy.

Winchester, like the rest of the country, was unable to escape the globalization phenomena that came about in the later half of the 20th century. As immigrants arrived to Winchester from Latin America, Asia, and other regions of the world, fresh faces started to emerge in the neighborhood. They initially arrived in search of work in the numerous factories and orchards that dot the city's landscape. However, when they established and started children, they gradually gave the city's culture a fresh, worldwide perspective. Due to this immigration influx, new religious institutions, ethnic marketplaces, and festivals honoring the rich tapestry of world customs also arose.

In addition, the second part of the century was a time of increased social and cultural awareness. Winchester's citizens began to perceive their neighborhood through a prism that was both more critical and more inclusive as a result of the influence of national movements supporting civil rights, women's freedom, and environmental stewardship. Institutions like the Museum of the Shenandoah Valley and the Bright Box Theater, which aimed to highlight a wide variety of skills and viewpoints, helped the local creative scene thrive. With the revision of educational curricula, students now have a more complete grasp of the world thanks to the inclusion of a larger range of history and literature.

Winchester had developed into a city where the ancient and new coexisted in a delicate balance by the time the new millennium arrived. Its population was an intriguing combination of recent immigrants from all over the world, families with African American ancestry that went back to the era of slavery, and early European settlers. This city's diverse population helped to create a thriving cultural scene that included anything from salsa dance parties to folk music festivals honoring the city's more recent Latino influences.

At the turn of the 2000, living in a city as diverse as Winchester was like browsing through a carefully managed photo gallery. Each page, each era, provided a unique glimpse, but they all added to a longer, more complex story. Whether it was the increase in racial and cultural variety, changes in gender roles, or the impact of other cultures, each development permanently altered the identity of Winchester. This is the chronicle of a community constantly remaking itself in reaction to the ups and downs of history, not just the story of population trends and cultural turning points. It tells the tale of Winchester's unwavering march into the twenty-first century while carrying a heritage that is as varied as it is rich.

Chapter 19: Post-9/11 Winchester

The terrorist attacks on the United States on September 11, 2001, caused a significant shift in the American psyche and altered how the country saw itself and its place in the world. The attacks on that dreadful day had an impact on communities all around the country, not just in New York City, Washington, D.C., and Pennsylvania, where they took place. Virginia's Winchester was no exception.

After 9/11, Winchester saw a more solemn and introspective atmosphere. Collective mourning and a swell of patriotic feeling were the initial reactions. Already a powerful symbol, the American flag gained much more significance. The Stars and Stripes were flying everywhere, from homes to businesses, serving as a visual reminder of community spirit and fortitude in the face of unfathomable loss. Church attendance increased as more people turned to their religious communities for solace and direction. Vigils and memorials were held, giving locals a place to gather, grieve, and start the laborious process of understanding the senseless.

However, the effects of 9/11 went beyond just the initial emotional responses; they also sparked a long-lasting change in a variety of spheres of existence. The attacks sent shockwaves across the economy, law enforcement, educational system, and even municipal government. Public safety and emergency preparedness quickly received new funding and focus. Like their peers across the country, Winchester's first responders underwent additional training to prepare for any terrorist attacks or major natural disasters. New procedures were devised for emergency evacuations, and public buildings underwent retrofitting to satisfy more stringent security requirements.

A considerable change also occurred in the political debate. Local elections and town hall meetings began to place a greater emphasis on national security. As the phrase "homeland security" spread locally, it changed how locals viewed their place in the larger scheme of national prosperity. The balance between personal freedoms and security was being reevaluated across the country as civil liberties and surveillance problems became contentious.

The post-9/11 era's pervasive sense of vulnerability has subtle but substantial effects on the social fabric of the neighborhood. There were more instances of friction and misunderstanding as 'the other', whether defined by race, religion, or political ideology, loomed larger than before. It's important to note, though, that Winchester also witnessed outstanding examples of interfaith and intercultural harmony. Discussions aiming at promoting understanding and refuting falsehoods were started by community leaders from various religious and ethnic backgrounds. Schools adopted instructional initiatives that promoted critical thinking about global issues and cultures, giving the next generation the knowledge and skills they need to succeed in the post-9/11 world.

The military community in Winchester was particularly impacted by a world that had been altered by 9/11. Local families witnessed the deployment of their sons, daughters, neighbors, and friends to other regions as the conflicts in Afghanistan and Iraq progressed. The fact that the country was actually at war carried with it a complex mix of pride, worry, and the unavoidable pain that comes with loss. Trees were decorated with yellow ribbons, care gifts were sent abroad, and local memorials received the names of the deceased. When veterans came home, they saw a community that was anxious to support them but was simultaneously struggling with the complicated issues of mental health and reintegration that such conflicts usually create.

The post-9/11 military engagements added yet another layer to Winchester's complex relationship with the concept of battle. The city's history is rife with violence, from the Revolutionary War to the Civil War. The city found itself thinking once more about the price of freedom and the sacrifices necessary to preserve it. However, this reflection's focus had changed as a result of the new century's global and ideological trends.

While the post-9/11 era brought difficulties and uncertainty, it also highlighted Winchester's resiliency and adaptation throughout its history. The city showed that it could change without losing sight of its fundamental principles by attempting to navigate the difficulties of this time. Winchester found a way to adjust with the times without losing what makes it special, whether it was in the areas of public safety, education, or community cohesiveness.

The 9/11 attacks continue to influence Winchester's collective consciousness more than 20 years into the twenty-first century, acting as a grim reminder of the vulnerabilities and obligations that come with belonging to a wider national and international community. Winchester continues to be, as it has been throughout its history, a microcosm of American difficulties and victories. It is always changing, yet it always remains rooted in the common experiences that give it its identity.

Chapter 20: Contemporary Challenges and Opportunities

Winchester is at a crossroads as we advance further into the twenty-first century, juggling the weight of its historical history with the dynamism needed to adapt to a constantly shifting environment. Winchester today is a city that exemplifies both the opportunities and the challenges inherent in the larger American experience, from social justice to environmental sustainability to economic diversity.

The city has a difficult task ahead of it in terms of its economy: moving away from an agrarian and manufacturing-based one to one that can support the booming fields of technology, healthcare, and service industries. Winchester must consider how to retrain its workers, adapt its industrial buildings, and draw new firms as factories become less active and farmlands lose their significance to the city's character. A number of programs have been started in recent years to support high-tech companies and entrepreneurial endeavors with the goal of transforming Winchester into a desirable center for innovation and thriving business. The city is also looking at joint ventures with neighbouring institutions and colleges to build an ecosystem that not only retains local talent but also creates jobs.

Winchester is weighing its environmental obligations in a time when climate change is a looming threat. The community is faced with issues that call for both urgent action and long-term planning, from the quality of the water in the Shenandoah Valley to the preservation of nearby parks and animals. Urban gardening, river cleanups, and educational activities on sustainability are becoming more popular, frequently in partnership with municipal governments. The debate of solar farms and wind turbines is becoming more prevalent in public discourse as the focus shifts to renewable energy options. A cultural shift and a reevaluation of the connection between Winchester's residents and the land they live on are also part of this multilayered battle.

Then there is the crucial question of social justice, a problem that reflects national discussions about inequality, race, and gender. These social processes are not unaffected by Winchester. Despite its vibrant, diverse community, conflicts nonetheless persist and frequently cross lines of economic inequality. Another issue with gentrification is the displacement of long-standing communities as newer, wealthier residents move into previously low-income districts, driving up property values. It's a transformation that both opportunity and conflict, therefore there's a need for complex solutions that can lead to equitable development.

Similarly, as residents discuss the fate of monuments and namesakes connected to a Confederate history, issues of historical memory and representation have entered contemporary discourse in the city. The city is struggling with how to respect its complicated and troubled past while also giving voice to tales that have been either disregarded or silenced. As locals collectively explore what it means to remember the past without becoming ensnared by it, museums, schools, and community forums have emerged as crucial spaces for these debates.

Even still, there are a lot of chances amid these difficulties. In addition to being a demographic fact, the city's increasing variety is a source of cultural diversity and social innovation. With the help of a wide range of voices that bring new perspectives to the stage, canvas, and written word, Winchester's artistic community is thriving. As the arts play a bigger role in the city's financial landscape, the transition is not merely aesthetic but also economic. Younger inhabitants are moving in, frequently attracted by career and educational possibilities, and they bring with them a liveliness and a desire to challenge the status quo, characteristics that could act as catalysts for significant change.

Technology, too, presents exciting opportunities for advancement. The use of telemedicine to increase healthcare access and smart city projects to improve local governance are just two examples of how technological improvements offer tools that could significantly enhance Winchester's quality of life.

One thing is certain as Winchester navigates these varied chances and challenges: the city is not a passive actor in its destiny. The city's institutions, citizens, and leaders are all highly conscious of the intricacies of contemporary life and actively creating the city's future. You may find a population that is really concerned about the welfare of their community in town halls, community centers, local newspapers, and even in casual talks at the corner store. This civic commitment is encouraging for Winchester as it looks to a future that respects its heritage while forging forth into the unexplored waters of the twenty-first century.

What leaps out as we close this chapter and wrap up our investigation is Winchester's persistent capacity for innovation, adaptability, and endurance. It's a tale that's far from over, as the city keeps changing in response to the fresh chances and difficulties that each day presents. Winchester continues to be a fascinating microcosm of America—its problems, its victories, and its never-ending search for a better tomorrow—for historians, locals, and interested outsiders alike.

Chapter 21: Famous Personalities from Winchester

Winchester has long been a place where people have made a lasting impression on not only the neighborhood but frequently on the country and the world. These notables, who emerged from Winchester's particular history and culture, give the city's development over time a human face. awareness the numerous ways Winchester has contributed to larger tales of American ingenuity, protest, and creativity requires an awareness of their stories, which comprise a crucial chapter.

Patsy Cline, the famed country singer, was possibly one of the most well-known people to have lived in Winchester. Cline was born Virginia Patterson Hensley in 1932, and she spent her formative years honing her expressive, passionate voice in the city's churches and other public settings. Her rapid ascent to fame was sadly cut short when she was only 30 years old due to a plane tragedy. She had a significant impact on both the country and pop music scenes, though. Cline became a trailblazing woman in the country music industry, and her hits "Crazy" and "I Fall to Pieces" quickly rose to classic status. The Patsy Cline Historic House, where guests may learn about her life and legacy, and where her legacy is kept alive today.

Willa Cather is unique among writers and journalists because she is a Winchester native. Cather spent her formative years in Winchester, where she developed her worldview and literary sensibility, even though she subsequently relocated to the West and is best known for her portrayals of life on the frontier. She developed a strong sense of place that can be linked to her early experiences in Virginia in pieces like "My Antonia" and "O Pioneers!" Themes from Cather's writings that are present in Winchester's own historical account include the pull of the land and human connections, which are also explored in great emotional depth in Cather's works.

The range of prominent individuals includes the political sphere as well. James Wood, a Revolutionary War officer who served as governor of Virginia from 1796 to 1799, is a significant character that cannot be ignored. Wood played a crucial role in the early growth of Winchester as a land surveyor as well as a political figure. His actions laid the foundation for the city's expansion, and his leadership during a turbulent time in American history established standards that would have an ongoing impact on the Commonwealth.

Similarly, Winchester-born Admiral Richard E. Byrd made an enduring reputation as an American naval officer and explorer. Byrd was a pioneering aviator who used new technologies to explore previously inaccessible portions of the planet and is best remembered for his journeys to Antarctica. His accomplishments went beyond individual acts of bravery to set scientific precedents that increased human understanding of the planet's most distant corners.

A discussion of Winchester's well-known figures would be lacking without referencing the accomplishments made in the fields of social justice and civil rights. People like Holmes Conrad, who gained notoriety as a lawyer and attained the position of Assistant Attorney General in the late 19th century, were crucial in the effort to overturn segregation laws and laid the theoretical foundation for the legal conflicts against racial discrimination that would peak in the middle of the 20th century.

Teresa A. Sullivan, a renowned sociologist and academic administrator, also deserves to be mentioned in a more modern context. Sullivan, who was born and raised in Winchester, has held a number of important positions, including the presidency of the University of Virginia. Her leadership embodied the principles of conversation, inclusivity, and justice, especially during school emergencies. She is a prime illustration of how leadership with moral principles and a strong educational foundation can be powerful agents of social change.

These statistics are the result of a community that has, over the course of its history, fostered inventiveness, ambition, and a sense of civic responsibility. They are not just isolated success stories. Whether they achieved prominence by their creative prowess, political sagacity, scientific discovery, or social engagement, these people were influenced by Winchester's cultural milieu while also leaving their own irreplaceable imprints on it. Their legacies are intertwined into the very fabric of the city, demonstrating how one person's life may shed light on a community's greater historical and cultural dynamics. These notable Winchester natives and descendants have made the city one that continues to capture our imagination and secure its position in the annals of American history through their diverse accomplishments.

Chapter 22: Winchester as Seen on TV

Winchester's appeal has penetrated well beyond its geographical boundaries, having an impact on popular culture and media, particularly television. Winchester has captured audiences around the country, allowing them to experience the city's distinct character from the comfort of their living rooms, whether acting as an actual filming location, an inspirational setting, or a backdrop weaved into plots. This chapter examines the ways in which Winchester has been portrayed and understood on television, as well as how these interpretations connect with the actual lives of its residents and popular imaginations.

Documentaries and news pieces that explore Winchester's extensive history, architecture, and cultural legacy have been among the easiest methods for viewers to learn about the city on television. These activities frequently include an educational component, whether they concentrate on Civil War sites or the city's significant part in different historical events. They raise the city's profile and establish it as a reference point for American history and culture. National networks like the History Channel and PBS, as well as local public access channels, have contributed to this kind of portrayal.

In addition to being the subject of real accounts of Winchester's past and present, the city has also been memorialized in fictitious TV settings, acting as a source of both inspiration and genuine storylines. The name of the city might be changed to give the writers more creative license, but anyone who is familiar with Winchester's landmarks and cultural quirks will frequently immediately recognize the resemblance to Winchester. Winchester is occasionally mentioned in TV dramas and comedies as a typical tiny American city that is both historically significant and facing contemporary difficulties, making it an engaging setting for the exploration of more general societal topics.

With the rise in popularity of criminal dramas and supernatural thrillers, Winchester has also found a home in similar stories, albeit frequently with a lot of creative freedom. While not necessarily accurate to the city's authentic character, these shows still give the city a sense of mystery and intrigue. They employ the city's historical sites and folklore as story points, adding levels of significance that, despite being made up, contribute to a larger picture of how Winchester is viewed by a wider audience on a national scale.

Also, Winchester has occasionally been used as a canvas for the projection of larger American concerns and aspirations. In this sense, the city takes on the role of a miniature version of America, encapsulating ideas like the effort to balance tradition and modernity, the benefits and drawbacks of diversity, and the difficulties of economic adaptation in a world that is changing quickly. Television shows that address these issues may use Winchester's rich cultural and historical context to enhance the depth and authenticity of their narratives. This allows the city to transcend its locality and transform into a lens for analyzing and comprehending larger American themes.

There is a two-way conversation between Winchester and the television characters it is portrayed as. While TV series use the city as inspiration, the resulting portrayals influence both regional and general impressions of Winchester. Numerous outcomes are possible from this. On the one hand, it can encourage travel and increase local pride. On the other hand, it might develop or support stereotypes that don't reflect what city dwellers actually experience.

Local responses to these representations can be complicated. While witnessing one's hometown portrayed on a big platform might be an occasion for pride, there is also debate about the fairness and truth of these representations. Whether locals believe these programs accurately portray their community or oversimplify it to the detriment of

Winchester, the impact of television on how people see the city is apparent. This interplay between a place and its media depiction is remarkable and illustrates not only how effective television is as a storytelling tool but also how it can influence shared cultural narratives and identities.

The impact of television on Winchester's cultural landscape is not only a transient phenomenon, but an enduring mark in the digital era where streaming platforms make these programs accessible long after their initial air dates. As viewers from all over the nation, and even the world, come to know Winchester through their screens, they interact with the city in a complicated, mediated interaction that enlivens, complicates, and occasionally threatens its rich history and diverse identity. As a result, Winchester's TV appearances transform from lighthearted asides to significant contributions to the city's continuous story, giving additional layers to its complex fabric as both a real-world location and a symbolic location in the American imagination.

Chapter 23: Winchester as Depicted in Literature

Winchester has a rich history of producing stories, both in the timeless form of literature and in oral traditions and local folklore. Authors have regularly used their pen to capture the spirit of Winchester's life, scenery, and larger-than-life stories, whether they are natives of the city or are inspired by its rich history and wide cultural palette. The city has been immortalized in books that span genres and time eras through novels, essays, poetry, and more, giving readers multidimensional perspectives that go beyond what is frequently depicted in history books or travel guides.

Let's take a look at the writing of the aforementioned Willa Cather, whose Winchester upbringing gave her a great respect for location and community, qualities she would later explore in her portrayals of the American frontier. Despite leaving Virginia, Cather's writings reflected a feeling for the interplay of place and identity that dated back to her formative years in Winchester. Even though her novels are not set in Winchester, the subtle depictions of social ties and the strong sense of place in her writing may be reminiscent of the Winchester experience for those who are familiar with the city.

Another unique perspective is provided by historical literature set in or near Winchester. For authors interested in this turbulent era of American history, the city's significance in the Civil War makes it a fruitful ground. Books in this genre explore the complex human drama, including the conflicts between families and neighbors, the challenging decisions faced by regular people, and the moral quandaries that resulted from a country at war with itself, in addition to illuminating the strategic significance of Winchester. These stories inspire readers to look beyond historical facts and figures and to immerse themselves in the lives of those who lived during these periods.

Additionally, current writers are interested in using Winchester as a location to examine modern issues including social justice, economic inequality, and cultural transformations. The city in these works frequently acts as a microcosm of America as a whole, much like in television portrayals. Here, Winchester serves as a backdrop for studying topics that are both current and timeless, such as the challenges of contemporary family life, the shifting nature of labor and industry, or the many facets of American identity in a society that is becoming more diverse.

Then there is the field of nonfiction and memoir. Winchester locals and those with connections to the city have written incredibly detailed tales that give readers a close-up view of daily life there. These works deepen and fine-tune our understanding of the city, whether they focus on the advantages and disadvantages of growing up in a small town, the difficulties of navigating identity in a place steeped in history, or the rewards and hardships of participating in Winchester's modern cultural and civic life. They serve as a reminder that the "real" Winchester is a community made up of people who all have unique tales to share, not just an abstract idea or a list of significant locations and events.

The complexities and subtleties of a location can be captured in literature in a manner that most other forms of art cannot. Deeper explorations into the inner lives of the people who inhabit a setting are made possible by this, offering details that are frequently absent from more plain historical or journalistic reports. The books, essays, and poetry that have been written about Winchester help us to comprehend the city better and on a deeper level. They join a group storytelling tradition that over time both reflects and molds Winchester's identity.

The literature about Winchester therefore offers a wealth of viewpoints, whether you are a local returning to familiar locations through the eyes of many narrators or an outsider attempting to comprehend the city's varied soul. With the aid of the written word, it enables readers to interact with the city in a discourse that transcends the present moment and touches on the past and the future. As a result, these literary representations of Winchester are incorporated into its ongoing narrative, serving as evidence of the city's enduring capacity to awe, intrigue, and capture the imagination.

Chapter 24: Iconic Winchester Landmarks and History

The city of Winchester itself acts as a palimpsest of American history, with each stratum revealing tales from various ages that have reverberations far beyond its physical bounds. This Virginian city is more than just a collection of structures or a collection of neighborhoods thanks to its blend of Colonial, Victorian, and modern architecture; it is a living museum that serves as a witness to the intricate web of occasions, movements, and people that have influenced it. Winchester's landmarks serve as focal points that anchor the city's history while enhancing its modern surroundings. These monuments range from Civil War battlefields to magnificent historical mansions, quaint downtown streets to cutting-edge architectural marvels.

The famous Winchester Courthouse must be mentioned in any discussion of Winchester's landmarks. The Greek Revival structure, which was constructed in 1840, is a monument to justice and government, but it is also a historical vault that holds a collection of tales from many eras. Its function as a hospital and prison during the Civil War reflects the city's turbulent involvement in that bloody battle. Numerous social movements and protests have taken place in front of its famous columns, which have witnessed the fight for social justice and civil rights.

The Stonewall Jackson's Headquarters Museum, housed in an 1854 residence designed in the Hudson River Gothic Revival style, is another significant historical property. The museum provides a detailed look into the life of one of the Civil War's most renowned and enigmatic personalities, Confederate General Thomas "Stonewall" Jackson, who used it as his winter headquarters from 1861 to 1862. However, it also brings up difficult issues related to memory, heritage, and the continuous discussion regarding how we remember and interpret the past.

The oldest house in Winchester, Abram's Delight, which was erected in 1754, provides a glimpse into the lives of some of the town's first European settlers for those who want to go even further back in time. This log and stone house is more than just a remnant of the past; it serves as a tangible link to the Quaker family who lived there originally, providing important insights into the daily lives, household practices, and labor conditions of the 18th century.

The Shenandoah Valley Discovery Museum is a totally distinct but equally significant type of landmark. Despite not having a historical theme, this interactive children's museum reflects the spirit of inquiry and curiosity that has long been a part of Winchester's identity. It demonstrates the city's dedication to educating the public and inspiring awe in the future generation.

On a different cultural note, the Patsy Cline Historic House serves as a reminder of Winchester's illustrious musical past. The iconic country singer Patsy Cline spent her early years in this modest home. It provides a window into the life of a lady who would later shatter countless barriers in the music industry, having been preserved and curated with extreme care. This residence honors Cline while also serving as a representation of the city's greater contributions to American music and culture.

Stylish buildings erected in 1924 that have been meticulously maintained to preserve its historical appeal, like the George Washington Hotel, are examples of contemporary landmarks that provide a window into the city's ongoing development. The ability of Winchester to preserve its past while excitedly embracing the future is represented by places like these.

These landmarks serve as cultural and societal touchstones rather than just being tourist attractions. They function as social hubs, learning tools, and locations for introspection. They contain tales of initiative, adversity, bravery, and transformation. They enable the city's past to continue to be a vibrant aspect of its present-day identity through their preservation and ongoing significance.

Each monument tells a different tale while adding to the overall story of Winchester, whether it be the seriousness inspired by Civil War ruins, the grandeur reflected in architectural masterpieces, or the thriving cultural life evident in its theaters and museums. Together, they paint a nuanced, multifaceted picture of a city that has been influenced by and is still shaping the American story. Each landmark entices you to turn the page and uncover the next layer of a tale that is as engrossing as it is illuminating, much like the chapters of a riveting book.

Chapter 25: Architecture of Winchester

Winchester's architecture resembles an outdoor museum because it displays the city's intricate historical progression in a vibrant montage of architectural influences, styles, and eras. While strolling through its streets, one may read the built environment much like a history book, with each building recounting a section of Winchester's broader tale and, by extension, the history of the United States as a whole.

Naturally, Winchester's architectural history begins with its early colonial buildings. The oldest house in Winchester, Abram's Delight, which represents the robust, useful architecture of the Quakers who first settled in the area, is one of the most well-known examples. The structure, which was mostly constructed from local logs and stone, is a relic of early American life and exhibits the simple yet efficient building methods of the period. It's far from grandiose or gaudy, yet it still serves as a reminder of the perseverance of the earliest inhabitants of Winchester.

The Federal and Greek Revival architectural styles started to become more prevalent in the city by the early 19th century. The Winchester Courthouse is a fine example of Greek Revival architecture with its imposing columns and symmetrical layout. Elegant yet practical, these structures frequently serve as notable municipal or institutional landmarks. These buildings are notable both architecturally and historically since they were frequently the locations of significant social and political events, in addition to being stunning examples of architecture.

Winchester entered the Victorian era in the second half of the 19th century, as seen by the presence of Queen Anne, Italianate, and Gothic Revival architectural styles. Victorian architecture adds a layer of complexity and flamboyance to the city's architectural palette with its detailed details, ornamental trims, and lavish color schemes. As an enjoyable contrast to the earlier, more restrained architectural forms, many residential sections exhibit the asymmetry and elaborate timber ornamentation typical of the Queen Anne style.

Winchester absorbed more architectural influences as the 20th century went on. The George Washington Hotel, which was constructed in 1924 and reflects the wealth and grandeur of the period, stands as a monument to the Beaux-Arts design. Its elaborate moldings, tall ceilings, and opulent interiors depict the spirit of a time when prosperity and artistic flourishing predominated. The functional designs of mid-century architecture, which are distinguished by clean lines and minimalist features, have a place in Winchester's landscape as well. These buildings exhibit the pragmatic post-war American attitude as well as some optimism and a forward-looking viewpoint.

Winchester has had a rise in modern and contemporary architecture recently, especially in the civic and business sectors. These structures, which frequently make use of steel, glass, and other contemporary materials, may appear to be a striking departure from the city's older architectural stock. They yet represent a continuation of Winchester's long history of architectural change—a willingness to accept the new without totally eschewing the old—in many ways.

One may see the city's mastery of architectural layering in the rehabilitation and adaptive reuse projects that have proliferated in recent years. With the addition of contemporary facilities, old structures are frequently given new uses while yet maintaining their historical relevance. This strategy not only preserves the city's architectural legacy but also improves modern day living.

Winchester's built environment, which has been influenced by wars, social movements, economic changes, and cultural influences, provides as a physical record of its complex past. Every design and building adds to the city's distinctive architectural fabric, providing a window into the past while continuously adjusting to the demands of the present and the potential of the future. Studying Winchester's architecture means participating in a conversation between tradition and innovation, past and present. This conversation helps us better comprehend the city as a dynamic, ever-changing organism. Winchester allows us to explore, reflect, and finally find our own position within its developing tale by telling it through its buildings in bricks and mortar, wood and steel.

Chapter 26: Key Industries of Economic Evolution

In order to comprehend Winchester's socioeconomic vitality, one must delve into the industries that have supported its development, highlighted its difficulties, and mapped out its potential for the future. A detailed analysis of Winchester's primary businesses offers an intriguing prism through which to comprehend not only the city's economy but also the principles, goals, and distinctive characteristics that have shaped it into a thriving component of America's economic landscape.

A crucial part of early life was agriculture. A large portion of the local economy during the 18th and 19th centuries was dominated by agriculture due to the lush, fertile areas that surrounded Winchester. The annual Shenandoah Apple Blossom Festival serves as a vibrant reminder of the significance of this fruit to the area. Orchards, especially apple orchards, find their roots in the terrain. The raising of livestock and the cultivation of grain were both important. These agricultural roots not only supported the city's economy but also formed Winchester's personality and morals by instilling in its citizens a strong work ethic and a deep sense of connection to the land.

Winchester's economy started to diversify with the coming of the railroad in the late 19th century. Transport was simple, which not only allowed for the development of industrial but also opened up new markets for its agricultural products. Winchester became a hub for mills, foundries, and other industrial endeavors thanks to its strategic location and burgeoning labor force. A cycle of expansion was sparked by the manufacturers, which in turn attracted a more diversified populace and further enhanced the city.

However, dramatic change only came about in the 20th century. Winchester switched its focus to service-based industries and advanced manufacturing as America did. New technologies acted as a spur for the expansion of industries like machinery, food processing, and plastics production. As businesses like Kraft Foods and Rubbermaid opened offices there, Winchester began to develop as a center for innovative manufacturing. Retail sales increased during this time period as well, which was helped in part by the city's advantageous placement along important transit corridors.

Another wave of economic diversification emerged in the latter decades of the 20th century and at the start of the new millennium. The fields of healthcare, education, and information technology have emerged as new economic cornerstones in Winchester. With its growing selection of academic offerings, Shenandoah University expanded beyond its original role as a university to become a key employer and contributor to the local economy. The Winchester Medical Center strengthened the city's standing as a healthcare destination by providing both employment opportunities and cutting-edge medical care.

Winchester serves as a modern-day microcosm of a balanced economic development. Alongside advanced manufacturing and emerging industries like IT and healthcare, traditional sectors like agriculture are still in operation, albeit in a modernized version. The blending of the ancient and new is a representation of Winchester's overall character, which is one of great reverence for the past and active engagement with the present and the future.

Winchester's emphasis on sustainable development is also noteworthy. Eco-friendly methods are being incorporated into a wider range of industries, showing a general awareness of environmental responsibility. Sustainability has emerged as a crucial element of the city's economic landscape, from clean energy options being investigated in manufacturing to organic farming methods gaining popularity in agriculture.

The adaptability of Winchester's economy was notably on display in how it handled difficulties like the COVID-19 epidemic and the economic recession of 2008. Winchester was able to handle these crises with a level of stability that many larger cities could be envious of thanks to a strong local economy, a diverse industrial base, and a strong community.

Looking ahead, Winchester appears to be in a strong position for future growth, thanks to its strong economic base, advantageous location, and unwavering innovation spirit. The city is prepared to adjust to the shifting features of the global economy because industries like technology and healthcare are showing great potential. Winchester will surely continue to change, as it has throughout its history, molded by the industries that support it while also adding its own unique flavor to the larger economic tale of America.

Chapter 27: Winchester in the National and Global Economy

Winchester's position in the greater economic fabric of the United States, and even the world, may appear subtle when compared to massive metropolises like New York City or Silicon Valley's high-tech corridors. This Shenandoah Valley city, however, offers an instructive case study of how smaller, strategically placed communities may have a significant impact on both the national and international economy. This is a tale about ties, flexibility, and the significance of place—aspects that are frequently overlooked in the more thorough explanation of economic evolution.

Even at the height of its agricultural prosperity, Winchester tended to extend its economic influence beyond the area immediately around it. Apples in particular were exported from the city to markets outside of Virginia, other states, and even other countries. With the growth of the railroad in the 19th century, its scope only grew. The ability to move goods over greater distances and more effectively allowed Winchester to transform from a largely self-sustaining farming village to a developing industrial center with more aspirational aims.

As the 20th century progresses, Winchester becomes progressively more crucial to the country's economy. Winchester quickly changed to accommodate the shift in American industries toward manufacturing. Businesses that developed facilities there included Kraft Foods and Rubbermaid, two significant players in the American consumer goods industry, in addition to creating work for local inhabitants. Winchester became an essential link in the nation's production and distribution network as a result of the extensive dispersion of the items produced there.

The fundamental shift, however, only became apparent as the global economy became increasingly intertwined during the last two decades. Winchester has proven to be adept at negotiating the difficulties of international trade and investment. In addition to hosting the activities of multinational organizations, the city has experienced the growth of its own businesses on a global scale. Companies with corporate headquarters or initial locations in Winchester have grown their clientele, supplier networks, and connections internationally. From cutting-edge manufacturing to IT solutions, Winchester-produced goods and services are a part of a larger, global economic ecosystem.

As a result of the large presence of educational institutions like Shenandoah University, Winchester is connected to international information and innovation networks. International teacher partnerships are frequent, and Winchester is attended by students from all over the world for their educational needs. This intellectual impact has significant negative side effects even though it has no immediate economic benefits. It makes Winchester a thought-leader, enhances the cultural richness of the region, and opens doors for future international economic partnerships and exchanges.

Additionally, how we see globalization as a whole is impacted by Winchester's position within global supply networks, particularly in sectors like machining and food processing. It serves as a case study for how smaller cities could continue to be resilient and relevant in a market that is becoming more and more dominated by global trade. The city serves as both a receiver and a transmitter of goods, money, and ideas as a node in these complex networks.

The issue of sustainability is a further issue that affects both domestic and global issues. A growing, global understanding of sustainable development is reflected in Winchester's rising emphasis on ecologically friendly solutions in a range of industries. These acts, whether they originate from local businesses using renewable energy sources or farmers engaging in sustainable agriculture, have an impact that goes beyond Winchester or even the United States. They are a component of a global dialogue about the future of the planet in which Winchester actively participates.

We can see a microcosm of many of the larger trends that have shaped our world over time by looking at Winchester through the lens of the national and global economies, from historical changes in manufacturing and agriculture to modern complexity in global trade and sustainability. The case of Winchester shows how, when strategically positioned and managed with care, even small communities may make significant contributions to larger economic systems. In this age of connectivity, Winchester plays an important role since its impact extends well beyond its immediate neighborhood.

Chapter 28: Notable Companies in Winchester

Winchester has always been a hub of creative efforts, creating an atmosphere that has fostered the growth of several companies. From its agricultural beginnings to its diverse industrial landscape of today, the city has fostered entrepreneurship and a resilient economy. The famous businesses that have had a significant influence on Winchester's economy, community, and beyond are examined in this chapter. These businesses reflect bigger trends while also influencing local conditions, serving as both reflectors and producers of Winchester's complex economic story.

The O'Sullivan Corporation is deserving of special consideration among the earliest industrial endeavors. It was initially established in 1896 to produce rubber heels, but it gradually expanded into producing various rubber and vinyl-based goods. O'Sullivan was a cornerstone of Winchester's industrial sector throughout much of the 20th century, providing hundreds of jobs and playing a crucial role in the town's economic structure. Even though the business eventually changed its location, Winchester can still claim it as one of the city's first industrial pioneers.

Since the 1980s, Winchester has benefited from the large employment provided by Kraft Foods, a well-known brand across America. The Winchester factory, which specializes in food production and processing, has been essential in supplying different food products to the national market. Not only has the presence of such a huge, well-known brand increased employment, but it has also significantly stabilized the city's economy. By participating in community initiatives, Kraft has strengthened its ties to Winchester and transformed it from a purely industrial presence to an integral member of the community.

Another prominent player with a long history in Winchester is Rubbermaid Commercial Products. Rubbermaid's Winchester factory, which produces goods for businesses and institutions, is essential to the company's global operations. Through its existence, Winchester has shown to be a viable location for modern manufacturing operations that service both domestic and foreign markets.

Shenandoah University is the shining star in the medical field. Shenandoah Seminary, which was established in 1875, changed through the years into a university that offers a wide range of undergraduate and graduate courses, including potent programs in healthcare studies. Shenandoah University is a major employer in the area and a center of academic activity because to its constantly growing campus and student body. Additionally, the institution attracts a temporary, multinational population that enhances the community's cultural and social life.

American Woodmark Corporation, a notable company that has risen to prominence recently, specializes in kitchen and bathroom cabinets for residential buildings. The business, which was founded in 1980 and maintains its headquarters there, employs a sizable number of people in Winchester. American Woodmark is a perfect example of how a local company may have a significant national impact because to its wide distribution of products.

The primary supplier of all-inclusive healthcare services in the area is Winchester Medical Center, which is a member of Valley Health System. The institution, which has thousands of medical experts working there, is a significant economic driver in the area. In addition to serving as an employment, Winchester Medical Center has established the city as a major regional healthcare hub by drawing patients from all around Virginia and nearby states.

Another noteworthy mention is Trexlertown Tech, a developing provider of IT solutions. This software startup, which was established in Winchester, has made progress in creating cloud-based solutions for small and medium-sized businesses. It serves as a shining example of how Winchester is more than just an industrial or agricultural center; it's also a haven for tech-savvy businesspeople.

These businesses are intertwined threads in Winchester's social and economic fabric, not merely standalone firms. They have facilitated community programming, sparked innovation, and produced jobs. They assist regional suppliers, add to the tax base, and may even work with nearby universities and colleges to build training programs. These businesses have transformed Winchester into a microcosm of the inventive and industrial spirit of the United States through their numerous achievements. Their narrative as a whole demonstrates how a mid-sized American city can support a thriving, diverse economy that endures despite the ups and downs of regional, national, and international economic trends.

Chapter 29: Visual Art and Movements in Winchester

Winchester's history is made up of more than just facts and figures, commercial success, or historical turning points; it also incorporates an ethereal aspect, probably best reflected in its long history of visual arts. Winchester is revealed as a location where the visual arts are both a mirror and a message, reflecting the town's soul while influencing its cultural story through the works of local artists, the sculptures that adorn public spaces, and even the architectural splendor that has developed over centuries.

Winchester's art scene was mostly shaped by lone artisans and wealthy families' patronage in the late 19th and early 20th centuries. Traditional artistic expression—landscapes inspired by the natural beauty of the Shenandoah Valley, portraits of important locals, and genre pieces representing daily life—marked these early years. The style was typical of the rest of America, but it gave Winchester a rich artistic tradition that would eventually motivate a more contemporary wave of artists.

A slow change began in the middle of the 20th century, most of it paralleling the larger changes in American art. Public art installations, art education facilities, and art galleries all grew in number as a result of post-World War II optimism, technological advancements, and a growing middle class that valued cultural consumption. Despite its modest size, Winchester did not fall behind. More modernist movements, like as pop art and abstract expressionism, also gained popularity at this time, profoundly influencing the local art scene. Artists like Frank Wright, whose ground-breaking works in a variety of media attracted national notice, came to represent this fresh, risk-taking mentality.

As the 20th century came to an end and the 21st century began, Winchester's art scene grew more diverse, incorporating a range of genres, styles, and cultural influences. The city started sponsoring biennales and art festivals that drew artists from the surrounding area and beyond. Murals covering the sides of buildings, showing everything from historical themes to abstract motifs, became more prevalent as public art. In addition to enhancing the urban environment, the public art pieces offered social and political commentary on issues including civil rights, environmental awareness, and neighborhood cohesion.

In documenting and presenting Winchester's artistic past, organizations like the Museum of the Shenandoah Valley have been instrumental. Their collections provide a thorough view of how the visual arts have changed in the area, spanning several centuries and artistic periods. These institutions' workshops and shows have developed into cultural icons that attract both locals and visitors while fostering the next generation of artists and art lovers.

Another important institution in Winchester's art community is Shenandoah University, whose Fine Arts programs provide as training grounds for new artists. Student shows are a common occurrence, giving budding artists a venue to present their work and network with recognized experts in the industry.

The global trend of digital art has recently had an impact on the art scene in Winchester. Local artists have embraced new media and technologies with speed, including video art, computer painting, and graphic design. This has led to a fascinating synthesis where traditional art forms coexist with cutting-edge digital expression, creating a kaleidoscope blending of the old and the modern in Winchester's art scene.

Winchester's visual arts scene is particularly fascinating because of how intimately it is related to the city's overall history and culture. A nuanced, comprehensive understanding of what Winchester is and what it aspires to be can be gained from murals that honor significant occasions or historical figures, sculptures that honor the city's apple-growing past, or modern installations that consider the region's long-term sustainability.

The visual arts in Winchester serve as an engaging storytelling medium by expressing the character of the town, the challenges and victories of its residents, and the beauty of its landscapes. It is a story that is constantly changing, adjusting to new influences and technology while always remaining grounded in the local, reflecting a community that takes great pleasure in its history while excitedly looking to the future.

Chapter 30: Music and Musical Movements in Winchester

Winchester's story is as much an aural one as it is a historical or industrial one. The musical legacy of the city is a moving illustration of its cultural mosaic; it is a melody woven from various strands that date back to its earliest settlers. Winchester's musical environment bears the marks of each age, weaving a tapestry of folk, classical, jazz, rock, and other influences. Winchester's music, a fusion of history and innovation that serves as the soulful background score to the city's continuing drama, must be heard in order to fully appreciate the character of the city.

Like much of America, Winchester's musical tradition was firmly anchored in folk and church music. Early Scotch-Irish and German settlers brought their customary hymns and songs, many of which related stories from mythology or everyday life. The main locations for such performances, where music functioned as both entertainment and a means of fostering a sense of community, were churches, community events, and family gatherings.

Winchester's culture was enriched by the introduction of blues and jazz components at the turn of the 20th century, as the Great Migration brought an influx of African Americans to the North. Despite not being a major center for these genres, the city's musical styles were undoubtedly influenced by their presence. Places like cafes and dance halls transformed into havens for musical experimentation, providing local musicians with the chance to jam with touring musicians, frequently resulting in exciting cross-genre collaborations.

Another change occurred during the post-World War II era with the popularity of popular music genres like rock 'n' roll and country. Due to Winchester's close proximity to other cities and the widespread use of radio, it was simpler for these new sounds to attract local listeners. The young people of the city soon formed bands, initially copying the music they heard on the radio but later developing their own distinctive sounds. The development of music festivals and free public performances—often staged in city parks or historic locations—in the latter half of the 20th century gave local musicians a platform to perform for a larger audience.

When discussing Winchester's musical history, it is impossible to leave out the Shenandoah Conservatory, a division of Shenandoah University. The conservatory, which was founded in 1875, has played a crucial role in developing musical talent and appreciation in the city. Its influence has spread widely, giving classes in everything from classical music to modern genres, acting as a breeding ground for new musical ideas. The Conservatory has also hosted a wide range of musical performances, from traditional operas to contemporary musical theater, enhancing the city's cultural calendar and bringing top-notch performances to the general public.

Winchester's modern music scene is thriving as ever, with its young population pushing the boundaries of musical expression. Independent bands, solo performers, and electronic music producers have discovered a supportive environment thanks to venues that are more accommodating of diverse musical interests. A growing hip-hop scene that incorporates worldwide inspirations and modern societal concerns testifies to the city's increasingly diversified population.

Also reflecting the city's involvement in the Civil Rights Movement and other social concerns, Winchester's music has made its way into the world of social activism. Local musicians have used their talent to advocate for causes ranging from social justice to environmental sustainability, demonstrating that music in Winchester is more than just an art form but also a means of communication and an expression of local ideals.

The musical history of the city is always changing, just like Winchester. The melody is a fusion of its history and present, resonating with the chords of conventional hymns, the rhythms of jazz, the disobedient tones of rock, and the avant-garde beats of modern genres. Winchester's music portrays the spirit of a town that is both proud of its history and optimistic about the future through each note and lyric. A constantly developing musical score, it enhances the lives of the city's residents and captures the essence of Winchester in each song.

Chapter 31: Other Cultural Festivals in Winchester

Winchester's social fabric has traditionally included cultural events, which serve as a vivid representation of the city's sense of community and its diverse population. Winchester hosts a variety of festivals throughout the year that honor everything from its rich agricultural legacy to the complex legacies of its several ethnic populations. These festivals go beyond simple entertainment; they are get-togethers that uphold tradition, promote community, and develop a rich discussion that enriches the communal experience and memory of the city.

Winchester's devotion to its apple orchards is best exemplified by the Apple Blossom Festival, which is maybe the most well-known of these events. The festival, a yearly tradition since 1924, has grown from a modest celebration of the apple-growing season to a lavish occasion with parades, a carnival, dances, and even a coronation for the Apple Blossom Queen. It soon becomes clear that this is more than just a festival as you stroll through the aroma-filled air packed with apple pies and blossom-infused treats that this is an annual reinvigoration of Winchester's agricultural traditions and community spirit.

However, Winchester's festival scene goes beyond apple blossoms. The city also holds a number of events that highlight its ethnic diversity. The Latino Festival, which brings the traditional music, dance, and foods of Latin American nations to the heart of Virginia, is a riot of color and flavor. The festival is more than just a show; it's a forum for cross-cultural understanding and appreciation of the legacy of various communities. In a similar spirit, the Winchester Greek Festival links the city to the Mediterranean region by bringing the flavors of moussaka, the sounds of bouzouki music, and the happy screams of "Opa!"

The Shenandoah Valley Civil War Era Dancers conduct an annual Civil War Ball, offering a singular chance for history buffs and the inquisitive alike to travel back in time. Although closer to its American roots, it is no less noteworthy. The ball is more than simply a dance; it's an immersive historical experience because it's held in historically correct settings, with period clothes, and uses music from the Civil War era. It also has educational value since it gives visitors a complex understanding of cultural life during one of the most turbulent eras in American history.

Newer, more modern activities have begun to appear in the community recently. One example is the Magic Lantern Theater Film Festival, which brings a selected selection of indie and foreign films to Winchester. This event democratizes the movie-watching experience and enhances the city's cultural offerings by converting everyday locations into pop-up theaters. Similar to this, the Shenandoah Arts Council frequently puts on arts festivals that bring together artists from various fields—painters, sculptors, musicians, and writers—to exhibit their creations and interact with the public, enriching the rich tapestry of Winchester's creative landscape.

The festival culture in Winchester is being shaped by everyone, even the young. Younger residents of the city actively participate in the city's rich social life, whether it is through school-initiated cultural fairs that seek to teach about and celebrate diversity or youth music festivals that feature local teen bands. These activities ensure that the spirit of celebration and unity is passed down to the following generation by providing young people with an early introduction to the benefits and obligations of community involvement.

These events are not just yearly occurrences; they are vital parts of Winchester's cultural fabric. Each occasion acts as a focal point and a platform for different facets of Winchester's diverse community to showcase their customs and skills. While adjusting to the modern world's evolving tastes and technologies, they serve as living museums, maintaining historical customs and beliefs. They help to break down barriers, promote understanding, and build a more cohesive community by acting as sites for cultural exchange. These events thus serve as snapshots of Winchester's changing identity, as well as celebrations of the past, the present, and the future.

Chapter 32: Key Educational Institutions

One of the foundational elements that supports Winchester, Virginia, is education. The city's educational institutions are regarded as hubs of community, research, and sociocultural development rather than just as places where young minds receive instruction. Every time a classroom is packed, a lab experiment is done, or a graduation is celebrated, Winchester's educational infrastructure is strengthened, further cementing its position as the region's epicenter of learning.

Shenandoah University is one institution that requires special consideration. Shenandoah Seminary was founded in Dayton, Virginia, in 1875. In 1960, it relocated to Winchester, and in 1991, it broadened its focus to become a university. Through its renowned Shenandoah Conservatory, the institution has contributed significantly to the cultural growth of Winchester in addition to serving as a cornerstone of the city's higher education system. The conservatory, which is renowned for its extensive programs in music, theater, and the arts, has influenced the city's thriving cultural scene by serving as a center for creative pursuits and top-notch performances.

Winchester is home to Shenandoah University in addition to a strong public education system. Schools like John Handley High School, which was established in 1923 and named for Judge John Handley, a supporter of public education, have a heritage that extends beyond merely being academic powerhouses. The Handley Library, which is frequently viewed as an extension of the school's learning environment, and the school's distinctive Beaux-Arts architecture make it stand out as a landmark in and of itself. Handley encourages an awareness for history, architecture, and the larger cultural context in which education is placed. It is not merely a place for textbooks and tests.

Another educational institution that serves a wide spectrum of students is Lord Fairfax Community College, which offers programs for people looking to advance their careers, earn an associate's degree, or use it as a stepping stone to a four-year university. By offering programs that are specifically designed to address the needs of regional industry, the school contributes significantly to the economy of Winchester by generating a qualified and immediately marketable workforce.

However, Winchester has a variety of community centers, workshops, and programs for vocational training that serve the local population, thus education is not just provided through official schools. For instance, the Museum of the Shenandoah Valley provides educational activities to aid both adults and children in understanding the history and cultural legacy of the area. In the meanwhile, workshops on sustainable living are held at the several community centers dotted across the city.

With their own unique educational philosophies and pedagogical approaches, private schools like Winchester Academy and Sacred Heart Academy give parents additional possibilities. By offering options that take into account various learning styles and belief systems, these institutions contribute to the educational variety of the city.

Not to be forgotten are the city's libraries, particularly the Handley Library, an architectural gem and haven for scholars. The library serves as a vital educational resource for Winchester by providing community activities, computer services, and a history archive in addition to lending out books.

These educational institutions have served as more than just classrooms over the years; they have also served as community gathering places, research hubs, and cultural venues. They have provided venues for discourse and creativity by hosting political debates, musical performances, art exhibits, and science fairs. By doing this, they have contributed to Winchester's changing identity as a city that appreciates both its past and its future by fostering an informed, involved, and creative populace.

Winchester is committed to building an atmosphere where information is accessible, diversity is celebrated, and community development is entwined with individual progress, as seen by the strength of its educational infrastructure. Each institution adds a distinct chapter to the continuous story of this vibrant city, acting as a key node in the complex web of Winchester's cultural, economic, and social systems.

Chapter 33: Winchester's Role in Academia and Research

Unbeknownst to some, Winchester holds a role in academics and research that is more significant than its small size might imply. This small Virginia town has a rich history, but it is also a thriving hub for academic research and innovation because to the collaboration of its educational institutions, regional businesses, and grassroots initiatives. Winchester's academic and research presence covers numerous fields, giving it a microcosm of intellectual vibrancy, from the labs of Shenandoah University to the busy activities of research-oriented businesses and healthcare organizations.

Without properly taking into account Shenandoah University, which has slowly grown into a center for academic study, one cannot discuss research in Winchester. Its programs in pharmacy and health sciences are particularly remarkable, where scientists do ground-breaking research on pharmaceutical efficacy, healthcare administration, and public health regulations. Many of these initiatives actively cooperate with Winchester Medical Center, giving theoretical frameworks practical implementations. In addition to doing research on performing arts pedagogy, the Shenandoah Conservatory of Music brings a special combination of creativity to Winchester's academic setting.

Furthermore, faculty members and students at Shenandoah University frequently work together on multidisciplinary projects that focus on the needs of certain communities. For instance, departments like Environmental Sciences and Business Administration have participated in projects to increase the sustainability of local agriculture. These joint initiatives not only give students priceless learning opportunities, but they also offer practical knowledge that helps the neighborhood and nearby businesses.

However, Winchester's academic community extends beyond the university's grounds. By encouraging a culture of inquiry among younger students, local public schools like John Handley High School make a different but equally significant contribution to research. The development of a research-oriented mindset starts early, with annual science competitions that entail challenging experiments and history projects that inspire children to explore local archives. Students are better prepared for further education thanks to this early introduction to research technique and critical thinking, which also fosters a passion of learning that lasts a lifetime.

The private sector is another indicator of Winchester's importance in research. There is a symbiotic link between regional industry and academic institutions as a result of the presence of businesses that specialize in biotechnology, materials science, and environmental sustainability. Internship programs, workshops, and team projects enable a smooth exchange of concepts, personnel, and assets between academics and business. The scope and effectiveness of research are increased because to this synergy, which also makes Winchester a desirable site for new and established businesses in tech-related industries.

Local government and nonprofit groups also contribute to Winchester's academic ecology by funding studies on urban planning, cultural preservation, and community development. Since the information gleaned from such study frequently informs the creation of policies, academics plays a crucial role in the administration of the city. These studies and reports are more than just static pieces of paper; they are active tools that legislators, local officials, and city planners may use.

In Winchester, research is more than just an academic activity; it is an integral practice that cuts across industries, enhances the neighborhood, and has an impact on daily life. Research activities in Winchester are felt in the city's classrooms, boardrooms, and living rooms, whether it be a university study examining the subtleties of Appalachian folklore, a high school project examining the effect of local policies on homelessness, or a business developing a novel clean energy solution. A new level of intricacy is added to Winchester's already complex story with every research article that is published, patent that is applied for, and community study that is finished. It enhances the city's reputation as a location where the past and present interact actively, driven by curiosity and the hope of discovery.

Chapter 34: Natural Disasters in Winchester and their Impact

The city of Winchester, Virginia, is full of contradictions; it is both historically and culturally significant and open to the whims of nature, which have occasionally brought it to its knees. Natural calamities, like as floods and storms, have influenced Winchester's infrastructure, policies, and sense of community. Even though they were devastating and catastrophic, these events helped the city become resilient and brought about transformational changes, so they now constitute a part of its living history.

With its wide rivers and lush surroundings, the Shenandoah Valley is both stunning and vulnerable to flooding. For instance, the flood of 1949 is remembered as a pivotal occasion that changed Winchester's attitude to environmental and urban planning. The Shenandoah River overflowed its banks as a result of torrential rainfall, flooding areas of the city and causing extensive damage. Even while the damage was considerable, it forced local authorities to reconsider their flood control strategies and make improvements to their drainage systems. Streets were raised, and zoning regulations were changed to prohibit building in flood-prone locations. The incident left a lasting impression on Winchester's collective memory and served as a lesson that encouraged more environmentally friendly behavior.

Winchester has also seen windstorms and tornadoes as a result of natural catastrophes. Winchester has experienced its share of violent storms that have put the structural integrity of both its contemporary infrastructure and old structures to the test, though not as frequently as in the Midwest. Reconstruction efforts after each incident frequently went beyond simple physical repair; they also led to evaluations of building rules and emergency procedures. In order to inform the public about safety precautions during severe weather occurrences, schools, hospitals, and other important institutions strengthened their disaster preparedness strategies.

Snowstorms have also had a distinctive effect. Heavy snowfall frequently disrupts daily life and presents difficulties for emergency services in an area where winters can be harsh. The city has been more prepared to face such issues with each passing year because to advancements in snow removal and road treatment brought about by the lessons learnt from each winter season.

Winchester has recently had to think about the bigger effects of climate change. The city has begun to include climate resilience in its planning as extreme weather events become more regular. There are many different strategies, such as improving the current flood defenses, adding green places that can absorb rainwater and lessen floods, and doing projects to lessen the city's carbon imprint.

Each natural calamity has also highlighted Winchester's social structure by uniting locals in acts of sympathy and assistance. These occurrences sparked a collective response that demonstrated the fortitude and compassion of Winchester's citizens, whether it was neighbors helping one another clean up after a flood, volunteers distributing supplies during a snowstorm, or local companies providing resources for reconstruction.

The most poignant example of how natural calamities have influenced creative and cultural manifestations that convey the general mood during those times is. Plays and songs, as well as memoirs, local newspaper articles, and photographs, serve as cultural archives for the experiences and lessons learned throughout these pivotal junctures in the city's history.

Each natural calamity has served as a kind of crucible, a time of trial that has changed Winchester both physically and psychologically. The city's response to these difficulties gives it a new facet of personality that is characterized by resiliency, ingenuity, and a strong feeling of community. Winchester has incorporated its history with natural disasters into its evolving identity, demonstrating its capacity to adjust and prosper in the face of difficulty. Thus, despite being upsetting and unpleasant, these events have been transformative, leaving a legacy that still has an impact on how Winchester views itself and plans for the future.

Chapter 35: History of Sports and Athletes from Winchester

When we think about all the different aspects that make up Winchester, Virginia's identity, its sporting history takes center stage. Winchester's sporting culture provides another lens through which to appreciate the communal spirit, values, and historical growth of the city, even though it is less immediately noticeable than its historical landmarks or academic achievements. In addition to assisting in the formation of local identity, this connection to sports has fostered athletes who have gone on to receive acclaim on the national and even international levels.

Baseball, the national sport, has a long history in Winchester, where amateur leagues have thrived since the turn of the 20th century. Bridgeton Stadium, which later changed its name to Jim Barnett Park, developed into a hub for the neighborhood, featuring everything from Little League games to matches between semi-pros. These events developed into social gatherings where members of the community gathered to cheer, commiserate, and celebrate rather than just watch the game. Baseball was quite popular in the area, and it served as a testing ground for potential players; some of them even made it to Major League Baseball.

Baseball is not, however, Winchester's main sporting attraction. Football and basketball have also made their presences known. Many of the athletes who have graduated from the local high schools have gone on to compete at the university and professional levels. For instance, John Handley High School has been a haven for talent, with its athletic program cultivating abilities while also imparting a sense of camaraderie and discipline that goes beyond the game itself.

The Shenandoah Valley's equestrian heritage and the city's diverse geographic topography are reflected in Winchester's sporting culture, which is notable for extending beyond the typical team sports to include individual interests like track and field, swimming, and even horseback riding. In addition to being a cultural landmark event, the annual Shenandoah Apple Blossom Festival also hosts a number of sporting events, such as golf competitions and 10K races, expanding the range of physical participation.

The success tales coming out of Winchester are motivating in and of themselves. Athletes have progressed through the ranks from local leagues to win state and national titles; some have even reached international competitions like the Olympics. But there are other notable individuals outside athletics. Coaches have made a substantial contribution to the regional and national athletic landscape, with many of them having lived in Winchester their whole lives. They've written plays that other schools have used, written books on athletic training, and some of them have even been honored for their coaching accomplishments by being inducted into local and national Halls of Fame.

Sports in Winchester have served as a mirror reflecting cultural changes, just like other facets of city life. Desegregating sports teams was a result of the integration of schools during the Civil Rights Movement, which in turn helped to increase societal acceptance. In part due to the larger national campaigns for gender equality, women's sports have also experienced a tremendous surge in popularity and support. The expansion of adaptive sports programs for people with impairments is a further indication of Winchester's dedication to diversity.

Sports events have frequently served as venues for altruistic endeavors, whether it is athletes participating in volunteer work in the community or teams raising money for regional charities. Along with winning, there is also a strong emphasis on giving back, which is consistent with Winchester's larger community values.

The economic, social, and cultural fabric of Winchester is knitted together with the historical threads of its sporting activity. Sports in Winchester are a communal affair, whether it's thanks to the support of neighborhood businesses, parental volunteers as coaches, or the inclusion of athletic training in a full education by the educational institutions. It's a thriving tradition that develops good citizens and athletes alike by instilling work ethic, self-control, cooperation, and a sense of duty.

The relationship between Winchester and athletics is not just one isolated chapter, but rather a continual saga that enhances the city's overall narrative as the essence of the place is captured. It captures the spirit of several ages, the aspirations of its youth, and the sense of community that has long defined this Virginian city. The next time you hear a baseball crack, a basketball net swish, or the cheers of a Friday night football game, keep in mind that you are not just watching a sporting event, but also an expression of the principles, culture, and sense of community that make Winchester so unique.

Chapter 36: Noteworthy Recreational Spaces

We have mostly concentrated on man-made objects and socio-political themes as we have traveled through Winchester's rich past, experiencing its heroes, architectural marvels, social movements, and more. But a city is more than simply its structures or its populace; it is also its parks, gardens, and other outdoor areas that give locals a respite from the bustle of the metropolis. With regard to the city's changing connection with the environment, public health, and community development, these recreational places each have a unique narrative to tell. These areas in Winchester represent the city's dedication to quality of life, sustainability, and shared experiences. They go beyond simple ornamentation.

One of Winchester's largest and most well-liked parks, Jim Barnett Park serves as a multi-use center where generations have enjoyed leisure time. It provides a wide range of amenities, such as sports fields, picnic spots, and swimming pools. The park's development reflects the city's evolving demands as well as its increasing understanding of the value of outdoor recreation and good physical health. Jim Barnett Park, so named in honor of a mayor who had a dream for a neighborhood recreation place, has developed into a welcoming location for a variety of people. It has progressively introduced amenities like dog parks, disc golf courses, and accessible play places for kids with impairments, demonstrating the city's flexibility and sensitivity to shifting lifestyles and interests.

Despite being primarily a place of learning, the Shenandoah University campus also provides additional recreational areas for the city. It is more than simply a refuge for academics thanks to its open spaces, strolling routes, and the Wilkins Athletic and Events Center; it also functions as a community area where events, games, and festivals frequently take place. It serves as a hub for town-and-gown relations as residents from all over Winchester congregate here for events ranging from soccer games to community festivals.

Winchester is a great starting point for individuals looking for more challenging outdoor excursions because of its closeness to the Shenandoah Valley and the Blue Ridge Mountains. Hiking, fishing, and camping options in places like the George Washington National Forest entice locals and tourists alike to experience the wonders of nature. These environments not only offer much-needed respite from the bustle of the city, but they also encourage a community-wide ethic of environmental stewardship. These unspoiled areas close to the city have sparked conservation efforts, educational projects, and even works of art and literature that appreciate the natural world.

Don't forget about the beautiful walking trails like the Green Circle Trail, which winds through various parts of the city and connects parks, residences, and schools. It's a linear park that encourages people to stroll, jog, ride their bikes, and even observe birds. It's more than just a route. Such initiatives show how innovative urban design has merged with a respect for natural environments to create a recreational network that improves Winchester's quality of life.

Community gardens have also started to figure into the story of recreation. Areas like the Abrams Creek Wetlands Preserve not only provide as a haven for local flora and fauna but also as outdoor classrooms for the general public and educational institutions. Here, a movement toward urban farming and community-supported agriculture gains traction, expressing a shared desire for sustainability.

These public areas serve as the "lungs" of the city, providing a location where residents may breathe more easily, think more clearly, and feel more connected to their surroundings and one another. These areas are multi-dimensional, providing something for everyone, whether it is the families who spend weekends playing by the lake, the retirees who find comfort in gardening, the athletes who work out on the tracks, or the artists who find inspiration beneath a canopy of trees.

In the past, Winchester's recreational areas have changed as the city itself changed over time. They have evolved from being only decorative elements to useful spaces, then to centers for civic involvement, and now, more and more, to custodians of environmental concern. They reflect broader changes in social mores, economic circumstances, and cultural fads occurring in the city.

Consider these leisure areas as yet another element of Winchester's complex personality as we draw to a close this chapter. They serve as the backdrop for first dates and farewells, senior outings and childhood recollections, intense athletic competitions, and quiet reflections. These public areas serve as stages for the everyday stories of Winchester, much like the theaters where plays are performed, the council chambers where choices are made, and the classrooms where futures are molded. They add to the ongoing story of a city that is passionately committed to the well and happiness of its residents through their presence and continued evolution.

Chapter 37: Noteworthy Nature in Winchester

As we dive deeper into Winchester, Virginia's complex tapestry, we discover that nature plays a significant role in molding not only the actual environment but also the personality and spirit of the neighborhood. The environment in and around Winchester provides more than simply picture-perfect backdrops; it also acts as a dynamic force, igniting wonder, luring adventure, and fostering a conservationist culture. The natural components that give Winchester its distinctive vibrancy and add to its feeling of place include the flora, animals, waterways, and geological formations that are the focus of this chapter.

The Shenandoah Valley, which borders Winchester to the west, sets the scene with its expansive meadows, agricultural regions, and views of the far-off Blue Ridge Mountains. For many years, the people of Winchester have found inspiration and sustenance in this magnificent valley. Agriculture has been encouraged by its healthy soil, and its stunning natural surroundings have attracted artists, photographers, and nature lovers. The issue of the delicate balance between human activity and natural preservation is one that has reverberated throughout Winchester's history, and the valley acts as a continual reminder of that.

In terms of vegetation, Winchester is proud of its trees because they not only have historical significance but also provide aesthetic and environmental benefits. The city is well-known for its apple orchards, and the apple has taken on some symbolic significance for the community. Orchards like Rinker Orchards and Marker-Miller Orchards are a part of a cultural tradition in addition to being profitable businesses. An important occasion in Winchester's social calendar, the Shenandoah Apple Blossom Festival honors this fruit and the arrival of spring with parades, arts & crafts, and public events.

The city is also endowed with a variety of indigenous flora that enhance the biodiversity of the area. The flora of Winchester is a constant source of natural education and enjoyment, from the dogwoods and azaleas in bloom that can be found in residential neighborhoods to the milkweed and goldenrod that draw butterflies and bees. Living displays of regional horticulture can be seen in gardens and green spaces like those at the Museum of the Shenandoah Valley, which frequently include plant species that have long been a part of the environment in the area.

Winchester's fauna is similarly fascinating and diversified, providing a window into the intricate web of life that exists there. Birdwatchers will find a wealth of species in the city, especially close to bodies of water like Abrams Creek and the Shenandoah River, such as cardinals, blue jays, herons, and occasionally even bald eagles. White-tailed deer, foxes, and raccoons are a few of the common mammals that can be seen. Their presence encourages discussions about coexistence and the value of wildlife refuges and corridors in an increasingly urban environment.

Another key component of Winchester's natural landscape is its network of waterways. The ecology of the area is greatly influenced by streams like Abrams Creek and the greater Shenandoah River. In addition to providing recreational activities like kayaking and fishing, they also provide as habitats for a variety of aquatic life. In order to maintain water quality and sustainability, groups and volunteers have focused their conservation efforts on these water bodies. They have organized river clean-ups and done educational outreach.

Winchester's natural story is further complicated by the nearby geological structures. Opportunities for both scientific research and adventure can be found in limestone caverns, karst landscapes, and the recognizable Blue Ridge Mountains. Hiking paths in the surrounding

George Washington National Forest provide views that capture the magnificence of the Appalachians, while well-known attractions like Shenandoah Caverns and Skyline Caverns enable tourists to explore an underground world of mineral beauty.

Winchester has grown more conscious of its obligation to protect these natural resources. Environmental protection and sustainability are the goals of conservation areas, educational efforts, and community-led projects. Environmental studies are incorporated into the curricula at the city's colleges and universities, generating a new generation of environmentalists. By actively involving individuals in projects like tree planting and animal monitoring, non-profit organizations and nature clubs foster a sense of community that is strongly rooted in the natural world.

In sum, Winchester's natural environment plays a significant role in the city's narrative rather from simply serving as a backdrop. It influences way of life, stimulates creativity, offers resources, and fosters a sense of awe and accountability. All year round, a silent symphony plays, giving a kaleidoscopic array of hues, a cacophony of sounds, and an infinite diversity of shapes and motions. As we explore the many facets that combine to make Winchester a charming and significant location, we must give nature a role that goes beyond that of a passive backdrop to one of a dynamic character that constantly improves the life and spirit of the neighborhood.

Chapter 38: Environmental Issues in Winchester

We discover that Winchester's relationship with nature isn't purely lovely as we continue to explore the city. Winchester, like many urban areas, faces a number of environmental problems that are both byproducts of its own development and expressions of more general, worldwide problems. These environmental issues, which range from worries about water quality to struggles with urban growth, from problems with waste management to the ever-present threat of climate change, push Winchester to consider moral, sensible, and even existential issues.

Let's start with the problems with Winchester's water quality, a subject that raises a number of complications. The city's valuable waterway, Abrams Creek, has frequently been the focus of pollution worries. Over time, runoff from highways, fertilizers from farms and gardens, and sporadic industrial effluents have tarnished its cleanliness. To address this issue, neighborhood groups and educational institutions routinely participate in cleanup initiatives and water quality inspections. Although the state and local governments have also put legislation in place to regulate pollution, recurring difficulties highlight the necessity for ongoing monitoring.

Another concern that has gained more attention as Winchester has grown is urban sprawl. The expansion of residential and suburban regions outside of the city puts strain on the ecosystems there and accelerates the clearing of farmland and forestland. The Shenandoah Valley's borders are being pushed against by the city's expanding footprint, which results in habitat loss and a rise in car-dependent lifestyles that raise greenhouse gas emissions. Planning and zoning regulations try to strike a balance between development and preservation, but the issue of how to sustainably manage Winchester's expansion is still up for discussion in the neighborhood.

The story of Winchester's environmental history is further complicated by the discussion of garbage management. Although recycling programs have gained popularity, there are still difficulties in efficiently sorting recyclables and informing the public about best practices. Additionally, much of the waste produced in Winchester, like in many other areas, is dumped in landfills. The issue of waste encompasses both home and industrial waste, and it frequently requires navigating complex legislation and neighborhood concerns.

Another issue is the often-overlooked quality of the air. There are days when air quality advisories are issued owing to increased levels of ozone or particle matter, even though Winchester may not experience the severe smog conditions that afflict larger cities. These frequently result from a confluence of automobile pollutants, industrial processes, and occasionally even localized natural occurrences like wildfires. Poor air quality has a wide range of negative repercussions, from short-term health issues like asthma to longer-term environmental damage.

Then there is climate change, a worldwide issue that affects every region of the planet, including Winchester. Both the natural and constructed environments are impacted by rising temperatures, erratic weather patterns, and an increase in the frequency of extreme weather events like storms and droughts. Local environmental problems could be made worse by climate change, which could further complicate water management, threaten native wildlife, and raise health risks from poor air quality.

A collaborative effort from numerous parties is needed to address these environmental concerns. The number of neighborhood groups advocating for the environment has increased in Winchester, and lively debates about ways to reduce the city's ecological impact frequently take place in public settings. To develop a better-informed populace, educational institutions in the region, from elementary schools to Shenandoah University, are progressively incorporating environmental studies into their curricula. Government organizations have been developing laws to support sustainable activities, such as encouraging the use of renewable energy and green building techniques.

Winchester's struggles with the environment are hardly exceptional; comparable problems are being faced by cities all around the world. The direction of Winchester's environmental destiny, however, is determined by local responses, influenced by individual acts, community initiatives, and legislative decisions. Despite the numerous difficulties, there is hope because of the increased awareness and active participation of Winchester's citizens. It emphasizes the idea that although environmental concerns are undoubtedly a part of Winchester's tale, they are not written as tragedies that must happen but rather as challenges that present opportunities for creativity, collaboration, and transformation.

Chapter 39: Technological Advancements from Winchester

Winchester's technical landscape may not be as well known as Silicon Valley's tech giants or Boston's biotech trailblazers, but it still has an interesting story to tell about constant innovation, adaptability, and reinvention. Winchester's history of technological development spans a variety of industries, from the early adoption of industrial methods in the 20th century to the city's expanding involvement in today's high-tech industries.

Winchester was mostly recognized for its agricultural production and conventional industrial businesses in the first half of the 20th century. Although subsequently relocated, businesses like the Winchester Repeating Arms Company's existence served as an early indication of the city's industrial potential. With the arrival of textile, paper, and electronics manufacturing facilities as the century went on, the area began to diversify its manufacturing base. In addition to creating jobs, these sectors also brought new technology that would pave the way for future innovation. The city's first significant step into technical modernization was advanced machinery for pulp processing and textile manufacture.

Due to its proximity to the capital, Winchester has become a center for government contractors and businesses in the aerospace, defense, and information technology industries. Because of this, enterprises could interact directly with authorities and win contracts that frequently required technology advancements in fields like sophisticated manufacturing techniques, telecommunications, and cybersecurity.

Winchester has had major advancements in medical technology over the past few decades, in part because of the presence of organizations like the Winchester Medical Center. Winchester has gained recognition in the larger healthcare ecosystem thanks to its research and applications in medical imaging, telemedicine, and health information systems. These medical centers frequently work with regional businesses and startups, transforming the city into a small but booming centre for healthcare technology innovation.

It is impossible to talk about Winchester's technological accomplishments without bringing up its expanding position in the renewable energy sector. Winchester has participated in programs centered on solar energy, wind energy, and even geothermal applications as a result of Virginia's commitment to a sustainable future. In addition to drawing businesses that specialize in these technologies, the focus on renewable energy has also prompted existing businesses to embrace green business practices, thereby fostering a circular economy of sustainability and innovation.

Another area where Winchester is progressively building a name for itself is in the field of information technology and software development. The city is now a desirable site for IT enterprises specialized in software as a service (SaaS), data analytics, and cloud computing thanks to the availability of a qualified workforce, supported by educational programs in regional colleges and training centers. This development has also been made easier by the availability of high-speed internet infrastructure that has been enhanced in part through public-private partnerships.

Winchester has reacted by investing in smart city technologies as the globe evolves toward a more digital future. In order to improve the responsiveness and efficiency of city services, initiatives have been initiated to integrate Internet of Things (IoT) sensors into public infrastructure, from traffic lights to waste management systems. These initiatives not only make life easier for locals but also act as model programs that other cities wishing to adopt technological solutions to urban problems might use.

Winchester's community and educational institutions are essential to promoting an innovative culture. The educational environment is focused toward providing future generations with the technological skills they will need in an increasingly complicated world, from STEM programs in public schools to specialist courses at Shenandoah University. A further layer to this fostering atmosphere is added by local hackathons, innovation centers, and business incubators, which provide venues for the testing, improvement, and commercialization of ideas.

In conclusion, Winchester makes important and diverse contributions to technical breakthroughs while not having the same international notoriety as other of the more well-known tech hubs. It is a city that is aware of how technology has a significant impact on social cohesion, economic success, and environmental sustainability. Winchester epitomizes American ingenuity—a tiny city with big ideas, constantly striving to better itself and the world around it—through its history of manufacturing and its expanding impact in industries like healthcare technology, renewable energy, and information technology.

Chapter 40: The Future Outlook for Winchester

It only makes sense that we think about Winchester's future as we come to a conclusion with this in-depth analysis of the city. Winchester faces a future filled with potential and challenges against the backdrop of a rich historical tapestry, the pulse of innovation, and a lively cultural environment. The perspective that follows is complex and makes an effort to frame the city's possibilities in a variety of areas, including economic growth, technical advancement, social progress, and environmental sustainability.

Winchester is positioned for economic growth. A strong foundation is provided by its broad industrial base, which includes both established industries like traditional manufacturing and emerging ones like technology and healthcare. Emerging industries present new opportunities for economic diversification, particularly in the fields of renewable energy and tech-based services. Winchester also continues to be a popular business hub due to its closeness to the Washington, D.C. metro area, which could lead to additional corporate relocations or expansions in the future. Making sure that this economic growth is inclusive and beneficial to all facets of society, however, is the challenge. For the city to be prosperous in the long run, it will be essential to address income inequality and create jobs for people with different skill sets.

Winchester has started to establish itself as a player in technologically-related industries like healthcare innovation, information technology, and smart city initiatives. With improvements in telehealth and remote learning as well as IoT technologies for effectively managing urban systems, it is expected that technology will become even more ingrained in urban life in the next years. Data privacy and cybersecurity issues will also become more prominent as the city continues to transition to a digital future. It will be crucial to strike a balance between technology advancement and moral considerations.

Winchester has chances to become a more welcoming and vibrant community on the social and cultural front. A melting pot of many cultures and ideas could flourish in the city as a result of shifting demography, enhancing its social fabric. But as we've seen in prior chapters, the city must also deal with persistent problems brought on by social injustice and past wrongdoing. Social cohesion can be sparked by ongoing discussion, inclusiveness-promoting programs in schools, and laws.

For Winchester's future, environmental sustainability is still another important concern. The city has progressed in using sustainable methods and renewable energy, as was addressed in Chapter 38, but climate change is still a significant issue. Some of the goals that will demand consistent work and innovation include developing resilience against catastrophic weather events, maintaining natural ecosystems, and moving toward a circular economy.

Winchester's future will surely be greatly influenced by education. A positive cycle of learning and innovation can be established by raising the standard of public education, expanding curricula to include additional STEM subjects, and encouraging collaborations between educational institutions and nearby businesses. Shenandoah University and other academic institutions will continue to act as intellectual centres in higher education, attracting talent and fostering research that might have broad repercussions.

To ensure that Winchester's expansion is sustainable and enriching for its citizens, wise planning is essential for urban development. Prioritizing mixed-use development can help address the problems caused by urban sprawl, while spending on public transportation could ease gridlock and cut carbon emissions.

In the end, Winchester's future is not decided; rather, it will be defined by the collective decisions and actions of its citizens and leaders. The city has demonstrated amazing adaptability and resilience throughout its history, traits that will be helpful as it negotiates the challenges of the 21st century. Winchester has demonstrated throughout its history that it is more than just a place; it is a thriving neighborhood with a dynamic narrative.

So, in ten, twenty, or even fifty years, how will Winchester look? Although no one can be certain, it is clear that the city is at a pivotal juncture. There are obstacles to overcome in every direction, but there are also fantastic chances for development, creativity, and advancement. Winchester is not a static monument to history, but rather a living, breathing being that is constantly evolving and striving, as we have seen in both its past and today. This steadfast character is what gives the city's future an exciting, limitless promise. As a result, even though this book might come to an end, Winchester's journey undoubtedly continues—it just shifts to a new chapter.

Chapter 41: Must-See Locations in Winchester

Location	Address	Reason to Visit
Old Town Pedestrian Mall	N. Loudoun St., Winchester, VA 22601	It's a bustling area with of interesting shops, cafes, and boutiques that makes for the perfect starting point for your exploration of Winchester.
Old Court House Civil War Museum	20 N. Loudoun St., Winchester, VA 22601	This museum, which is conveniently situated on the Old Town Pedestrian Mall, offers a detailed look at Civil War history.
Museum of the Shenandoah Valley	901 Amherst St., Winchester, VA 22601	A extensive museum with gorgeous gardens to wander through and information on the history, culture, and art of the region.
Handley Regional Library	100 W. Piccadilly St., Winchester, VA 22601	Even if you're not a reader, the Beaux-Arts architecture is stunning and well worth seeing. The pedestrian mall is nearby.
Patsy Cline Historic House	608 S. Kent St., Winchester, VA 22601	Fans of country music should visit this historic home, which offers a close-up look into the life of a legendary musician.
Jim Barnett Park	1001 E. Cork St., Winchester, VA 22601	If you wish to reconnect with nature, this park has paths, recreational opportunities, and gorgeous open spaces.
Abrams Creek Wetlands Preserve	Abrams Creek Dr., Winchester, VA 22601	Ideal for a brief, easy hike where you can see uncommon plant and bird species.
Christ	211 S.	a lengthy history, beautiful yard, and a

Location	Address	Reason to Visit
Episcopal Church	Center St., Winchester, VA 22601	tranquil retreat with stained glass windows.
Winchester Brew Works	320 N. Cameron St., Winchester, VA 22601	After a day of sightseeing, stop by this neighborhood brewery that serves craft brews for a relaxing atmosphere.
Stonewall Jackson's Headquarters	415 N. Braddock St., Winchester, VA 22601	An important book on the Civil War that provides insight into the strategies and life of Confederate General Stonewall Jackson.

Don't miss out!

Visit the website below and you can sign up to receive emails whenever Henry Church publishes a new book. There's no charge and no obligation.

https://books2read.com/r/B-A-GDIAB-RMAOC

BOOKS 2 READ

Connecting independent readers to independent writers.

Also by Henry Church

American Cities History Guidebook Series
Charlottesville, Virginia: Historical Guide for Travelers
Williamsburg, Virginia: Historical Guide for Travelers
Richmond, Virginia: Historical Guide for Travelers
Norfolk & Virginia Beach: Historical Guide for Travelers
Winchester, Virginia: Historical Guide for Travelers
Baltimore, Maryland: Historical Guide for Travelers
Dover, Delaware: Historical Guide for Travelers
Arlington, Virginia: Historical Guide for Travelers

About the Publisher

Fiel LLC is dedicated to providing high-quality content at affordable prices, utilizing state-of-the-art processes and advanced content generation systems to ensure a superior reading experience. All books published by Fiel LLC are for entertainment purposes only. Fiel LLC authors use pen names and are not experts in any field, so no content should be taken as financial, medical, legal, or professional advice. All information provided is subject to change, and readers are encouraged to verify the latest details through their own research.